CREDIT WHERE IT'S DUE

CREDIT WHERE IT'S DUE

Rethinking Financial Citizenship

Frederick F. Wherry,
Kristin S. Seefeldt, and
Anthony S. Alvarez

Russell Sage Foundation
New York

The Russell Sage Foundation

The Russell Sage Foundation, one of the oldest of America's general purpose foundations, was established in 1907 by Mrs. Margaret Olivia Sage for "the improvement of social and living conditions in the United States." The foundation seeks to fulfill this mandate by fostering the development and dissemination of knowledge about the country's political, social, and economic problems. While the foundation endeavors to assure the accuracy and objectivity of each book it publishes, the conclusions and interpretations in Russell Sage Foundation publications are those of the authors and not of the foundation, its trustees, or its staff. Publication by Russell Sage, therefore, does not imply foundation endorsement.

Library of Congress Cataloging-in-Publication Data

Names: Wherry, Frederick F., author. | Seefeldt, Kristin S., author. | Alvarez, Anthony S., author.
Title: Credit where it's due : rethinking financial citizenship / Frederick F. Wherry, Kristin S. Seefeldt, and Anthony S. Alvarez.
Description: New York : Russell Sage Foundation, [2019] | Includes bibliographical references and index.
Identifiers: LCCN 2018044087 (print) | LCCN 2018058819 (ebook) | ISBN 9781610448840 (ebook) | ISBN 9780871548665 (pbk. : alk. paper)
Subjects: LCSH: Consumer credit.
Classification: LCC HG3755 (ebook) | LCC HG3755 .W445 2019 (print) | DDC 332.7/43—dc23
LC record available at https://lccn.loc.gov/2018044087

The paper used in this publication meets the minimum requirements of American National Standard for Information Sciences—Permanence of Paper for Printed Library Materials. ANSI Z39.48-1992.

Text design by Suzanne Nichols.

Cover photo © Martha Nichols.

RUSSELL SAGE FOUNDATION
112 East 64th Street, New York, New York 10065
10 9 8 7 6 5 4 3 2 1

Contents

About the Authors |

FREDERICK F. WHERRY is professor of sociology at Princeton University.

KRISTIN S. SEEFELDT is associate professor of social work and public policy at the University of Michigan, Ann Arbor.

ANTHONY S. ALVAREZ is assistant professor of sociology at California State University, Fullerton.

Foreword |

Consumers in America today have access to a dazzling array of tools powered by the latest technologies to help track and manage their financial lives. They are also backed by a $55 billion industry of financial planners ready to advise them on everything from mixing investments for optimum returns to planning for retirement.[1] Although these services are largely targeted at people of means, the United States also spends $670 million annually on financial education for people with far fewer resources through programs at public schools and nonprofit organizations.[2]

Despite this reality, financial wellness is still elusive for millions of Americans. A Consumer Financial Protection Bureau (CFPB) report on financial well-being found that about one-third of individuals in the United States have difficulty making ends meet and that approximately one in five struggle to afford basic needs like food, housing, and medical care.[3] Given the complexity of the issue, the CFPB report could not attribute people's financial insecurity to any one factor alone but rather noted the impact of many interrelated factors.

Financial well-being is about more than just how well individuals manage their money. Normally, we think that a person's financial life is the sum of his or her financial decisions and knowledge of spending, saving, and investing. Conventional wisdom has us believing that individuals determine their own financial well-being, all else being equal. But all is not equal, or normal, in America.

Society plays a role in determining people's financial lives, guided in no small part by the notions of "belonging" and "othering." Professor john a. powell and Stephen Menendian explain that *belonging* "confers the privileges of membership in a community, including the care and concern of other members," while *othering* "marginalize[s] people on the basis of perceived group differences," rendering them outside the circle of concern. These notions of belonging and othering are so ingrained that they form the basis for policies that invest in and appropriate resources to people we deem to belong, while at the same time extracting from and exploiting those we perceive as the other.[4] These ideas in many ways determine the winners and losers in our financial systems.

The financial consequences for people perceived as other are truly devastating. In the 1930s, for example, the Home Owners' Loan Corporation, a government-sponsored corporation created to help homeowners refinance mortgages in default and prevent foreclosure, mapped neighborhoods comprising predominantly people of color in red ink to signal "infestations" of "Negroes," "Orientals," or "foreigners."[5] Mortgage lenders then used those maps as grounds to deny loans—closing off sources of capital to residents looking to improve their homes—and demand higher mortgage rates from some prospective buyers. For decades, so-called redlining in communities of color severely diminished the appreciation of homes, the major source of wealth for most working Americans to this day. This policy also had the inverse effect in predominantly white neighborhoods of increasing demand for homes, their value, and residents' wealth.

Wealth-stripping based on discrimination and othering is not limited to mortgages, nor is it a thing of the past. In many communities today, fees and fines disproportionately hurt people of color. In 2015, the U.S. Department of Justice released the Ferguson Report, which found police departments and municipal courts guilty of charging high court fines on nonviolent offenses like traffic violations, arresting people who could not pay, and referring unpaid fees to collection agencies, a practice that inflicts enduring financial harm by leaving negative marks on individuals' credit reports.[6]

The Ferguson Report sparked similar investigations all over the country. The Lawyers' Committee for Civil Rights found that four million Californians have had their driver's licenses suspended for inability to pay court-ordered fines and tickets.[7] The authors of that report noted, "These suspensions make it harder for people to get and keep jobs, further impeding their ability to pay their debt. They harm credit ratings. They raise public safety concerns. Ultimately, they keep people in long cycles of poverty that are difficult, if not impossible, to overcome."[8]

Other reports have found similar patterns of discrimination and financial injustice against the "other." A New America Foundation report noted that community banks charge people of color more for opening and maintaining basic entry-level checking accounts. In total, the report concludes, the average fees are $25.53 higher for Asians, $190.09 higher for blacks, and $262.09 higher for Latinx than for whites.[9]

Because notions of belonging and othering inform the policies that frame our social and economic systems, they ultimately determine people's financial futures. Fortunately, these concepts are not fixed, but flexible:

they can expand or contract with social, political, and demographic pressures. America's suffrage, civil rights, and immigrant rights movements are but a few examples of successful efforts to expand our collective circle of concern.

History can be easily forgotten when we turn our attention to perfecting a set of products to help people achieve financial security. Ignoring the social and political dimensions of financial well-being might lead us to build tools that simply reinforce the status quo. Without intentionally challenging the exclusion and criminalization of people who are poor, people of color, and immigrants, our work will be forever incomplete. So too if we do not see the fullness of people themselves, recognize their agency as human beings, and honor their creativity and freedom of choice.

Despite enormous obstacles, people at the margins find ways to manage their financial needs and obligations. What can we learn from their innovative strategies to survive? At Mission Asset Fund (MAF), this fundamental question guides our work with the people we serve: those living in the shadows of mainstream financial systems today. We reject the traditional, worn-out, deficit-based approach that looks at clients as broken, ignorant, and insufficient. Instead, we lift up their strengths as the starting point of engagement. We meet our clients where they are, and we build solutions based on respect for what is already inherently good in their lives.

This values-driven approach allows us to see and appreciate what our clients typically do with their money. Immigrants, for example, have a rich, time-honored tradition of coming together to lend and save resources in groups of trusted family and friends. We built our lending circles program on this informal practice, turning what are known as tandas, susus, or cundinas into financial products that institutions can understand. Lending circle participants sign promissory notes allowing MAF to service and report loan activity to credit bureaus, thereby helping these clients establish or improve their credit scores. We are using the best of finance and technology for good, creating culturally relevant programs and sharing insights to expand the notion of belonging in America.

There is much we need to learn from those at the margins of society today. I am grateful to Professors Frederick Wherry, Kristin Seefeldt, and Anthony Alvarez for working with us to unearth even more insights into the financial lives of our clients.

My decades-long friendship with Dr. Wherry proved to be the starting point for this particular project. We first met in 1994 during a summer program designed to expose college students of color to careers in public policy. We met again years later as graduate students at the Woodrow Wilson School. There we took a small reading course with Professor Alejandro Portes. Our respective career paths were transformed as a result. Now, after twenty years, we have teamed up again, this time to listen and learn from MAF clients about their financial lives.

What we found is just how meaningful debt and credit are for people trying to belong. People yearn to have meaningful relationships, to be seen fully, to be treated with respect and dignity. But cast as the other and confronting barriers to legal status and citizenship, millions of immigrants are blocked from living up to their full potential and their financial security becomes ever more difficult to achieve. Despite the cloud of uncertainty hanging over their lives, they do not give up—they find ways to move forward.

Just like the millions of immigrants who came before them, people today want opportunities to realize the American Dream. They still arrive with that belief that anyone who works hard and contributes meaningfully—who plays by rules that are just and fair—can share in America's prosperity. For immigrants, realization of the American Dream might be symbolized through home or business ownership. It could mean having a better life than their parents did, or their children reaching even higher, attaining a true sense of wellness, financial and otherwise. All of us in this country stand to benefit when this occurs, but people today need more than cutting-edge financial tools or savvy advisers to realize the American Dream. They need to belong.

José A. Quiñonez
Mission District, San Francisco, California

Acknowledgments |

THIS BOOK COULD not have been written without José Quiñonez, the founder and CEO of Mission Asset Fund, as well as the MAF staff and clients. Doris Vasquez made us all feel welcomed and was instrumental in helping us line up interviews. Aparna Ananthasubramaniam managed the recruitment and transcription process out of the MAF office. Other staff who were helpful include Daniela Salas, Tara Robinson, Mohan Kanungo, Daniel Lau, Miguel de la Fuente-Lau, Jeremy Jacob, and Joel Lacayo.

We gratefully acknowledge the support of the Behavioral Economics Program at the Russell Sage Foundation, the encouragement of its president, Sheldon Danziger, and the caring guidance of Suzanne Nichols, director of the Russell Sage Foundation press. MAF also received research support from JP Morgan Chase & Co. to help with data collection efforts.

Tomás Jimenez at Stanford helped us find an excellent research assistant, Marlene Orozco. And Ross Advincula and John Moon opened their home to reduce hotel stays when Fred Wherry was observing MAF staff at work.

At our home institutions, Fred Wherry received significant financial support from the Sociology Department and the Provost Office of Yale University and from the Sociology Department and the Science Fund at Princeton University; Kristin Seefeldt from the School of Social Work at the University of Michigan; and Anthony Alvarez from the Department of Sociology at California State University at Fullerton. We benefited from the copyediting prowess of Irina Oryshkevich as we reconciled our three voices into a seamless narrative. And we thank Mitch Duneier for advice and support as the narrative came together.

The anonymous reviewers at the Russell Sage Foundation deserve a special word of thanks. They carefully engaged our work and pushed us to make it better.

Our respective families deserve more gratitude than we are able to express. They have encouraged us, put up with us, and reminded us that social science can be put to good use.

Prologue |

WHEN WE BEGAN working on this book, our intention was to focus on the Mission Asset Fund and document what happens when financial institutions recognize the positive financial behavior of people of color. Such behavior, apparent but unacknowledged, has not helped people of color obtain loans on reasonable terms, if at all. As José Quiñonez, founder of the Mission Asset Fund, explained, "We knew that people of color and others around the globe have been using rotating savings and credit associations (ROSCAs) and engaging in other informal financial practices for a long time. We got so focused on the savings part of it that we didn't examine its credit side enough. People were reliably paying their weekly or monthly loan obligations in ways similar to how they would pay a credit card bill. Why, then, were these activities not showing up in their credit reports?"[1] By formalizing ROSCAs and informing credit reporting bureaus of on-time payments, the Mission Asset Fund has helped this population receive recognition for practices that demonstrate its reliability in financial matters.

"As we were initially designing MAF's programs, I found myself thinking back to my time at Princeton, where I learned about informal economies, the economic activity that goes on outside the regulated system," wrote Quiñonez, who earned his master's from Princeton's Woodrow Wilson School.[2] It was there that he was introduced by Alejandro Portes, a professor (now emeritus) of sociology and public affairs, to a robust literature on social capital and community development and learned about immigrants who had mobilized remittances for private consumption and public works. Quiñonez was also inspired by Hernando de Soto's writings on the enormity of unreported, unrecorded economic practices. "In the developing world," Quiñonez points out,

> lots of poor people have property, often because they were born in the same house as their parents, but many of them may not have title to their property. Without that piece of paper proving that the asset belongs to them, it is

difficult for them to participate in the formal economy, which could otherwise open up new opportunities. For example, without proof of ownership they can't use their property as collateral for a loan to start a business. They can't bequeath their home to their children. They can't even sell it. Their asset is essentially invisible.[3]

The same holds true for credit scores and financial capability: new possibilities can be unleashed only if policymakers and private-sector actors are willing to see the indicators of value in stigmatized places and persons. At the Mission Asset Fund, Quiñonez merged Portes's and de Soto's ideas to make the invisible visible within the financial system and thus give people credit for the good things they had already done or were doing.

Had this been the entire story, it would have been enough. However, as we interviewed MAF's clients and observed the staff in action, we discovered far more. From this tale of economic empowerment, we extracted a framework for financial citizenship, experienced from the ground up. As we sketched out its details, we began to realize that financial citizenship underlies a range of discussions regarding financial inclusion and financial well-being.

The political theorist Danielle Allen has likewise challenged our understanding of equality and inclusion, but in the context of education.[4] What does political equality mean for the types of educational opportunities made available to individuals? What are the implications for individuals who co-create the very institution in which they seek inclusion? We ask similar questions about household finance. Like Allen, we have found that financial citizenship is blocked when decisions made by individuals are not viewed by the mainstream as legitimate and when they are prevented from pursuing and creatively coproducing their communities and institutions. How can individuals affirm their dignity and the dignity of others when their right to feel a sense of belonging in a particular group or to participate in financial organizations in their neighborhood goes unrecognized? And what, finally, can be done for those groups of people who continue to be treated as separate and unequal?

With these questions, we aim to change the conversation on the meaning of credit and debt in the lives of the disadvantaged. Keep in mind that the overall economy is not yet inclusive, just as our overall political system is not yet just. In this book, we shine a light on the Mission Asset Fund as an example of what the move toward justice looks like from below and to inquire about the policy changes that will be required from above. We invite our readers to accompany us on that quest.

Introduction | Separate and Unequal

THOUGH RAISED IN post–civil rights America, Marisol was living in a separate and unequal world. She earned a steady income and had gone to community college. Yet despite paying most of her bills on time, she was invisible; she had no credit score. Having left her boyfriend, she was looking for a place in a safe neighborhood that she could call home for herself and her daughter. This was when she first encountered landlords who ran credit checks. Some of them also demanded more than the first and last month's rent as deposit because they weren't sure whether they could trust her. Others simply said no. Was it fair that so much was expected from one to whom so little had been given?

Anticipating frustration or humiliation, credit-invisibles like Marisol sometimes opt for lower-quality housing in "undesirable" and underserved neighborhoods, where their official credit histories are far less likely to face close scrutiny. Others, finding themselves upwardly mobile despite their lack of a credit score, may decide to purchase a modest home as they pursue the American Dream. They too, however, find themselves treated unequally, often paying considerably more for the same home than someone with decent credit would pay. For an individual with a subprime credit score, a mortgage debt of $100,000, for example, can easily amount to an extra $70,000 over the life of the loan, leaving that much less to invest in a 401(k) retirement account or college fund or as a startup fund for a business.[1] It might seem fair to charge people according to the risk they pose and their chances of defaulting. But what if such an assessment is based on flawed information? What if the behaviors indicating that these individuals can pay on time and in fact are a relatively low risk for defaulting are simply ones that the credit reporting bureaus are not tracking? In other words, why should consumers have debilitating credit scores that do not reflect their actual behavior and potential actions?

In the eyes of employers, good credit signals not simply the likelihood of repayment but also—and increasingly—moral character (reliability,

1

punctuality, reasonableness). Just as job applications ask potential employees to "check the box" if they have a criminal record, they sometimes ask them to fill in a different box for permission to run a credit check. For those with low credit scores or none at all, a strong work ethic and proper work experience may not be enough to get a job, and if they do get a job, a low credit score may prevent them from obtaining a timely promotion. In short, the pursuit of safety, employment, and social recognition relies increasingly on maintaining a good credit score.

Credit invisibility reflects existing racial inequalities. An estimated 45 million adults in the United States lacked a credit score in 2010—either because they had no credit history or because they had too few active lines of credit to be scored—but the burden fell hardest on blacks and Latinx (28 percent in both cases), in contrast to Asians (17 percent) and whites (16 percent), depicted here in figure I.1.[2] The disadvantages of credit invisibility compound the existing racial inequalities from which they spring. The sociologists Rourke O'Brien and Barbara Kiviat conducted a survey experiment involving 1,050 hiring professionals and found that when otherwise equally qualified applicants had a bad credit score, a lower starting salary was recommended for blacks than for whites, and for women compared to men.[3]

Bipartisan partnerships in Congress have made an effort to remedy unjust denials of visibility. The policy agenda focuses on fixing market failures caused by information asymmetries and the correction of human failures generated by cognitive biases. For example, while promoting the Credit Access and Inclusion Act (H.R. 4172), Democratic congressman Keith Ellison of Minnesota and Republican congressman Michael Fitzpatrick of Pennsylvania argued that it is unfair that some people who are just as likely to repay a debt on time as other people nonetheless receive different loan terms and higher interest rates on their credit cards simply because regulators have prevented credit scoring agencies from obtaining relevant information about them. Financial service providers lack the necessary information to offer lower-cost loans to people whose financial histories are harder to collect. If that information could be gathered more effectively, more people would have access to fair loan terms and interest rates. Those with similar capacities would then have the same opportunities to participate in financial services and social life.

Though welcome, these calls for financial inclusion may make the very outcomes they seek less likely. The notion of financial inclusion proffered in the halls of Congress implicitly places the economy, politics, and social life in separate spheres. The separate and unequal distribution of debt and credit, in the economic view, results from nothing other than information asymmetry, revealed preferences, cognitive biases, and lack of willpower.

Figure I.1   U.S. Adults Considered Credit-Invisible or Having No
Credit Score, by Race, 2010

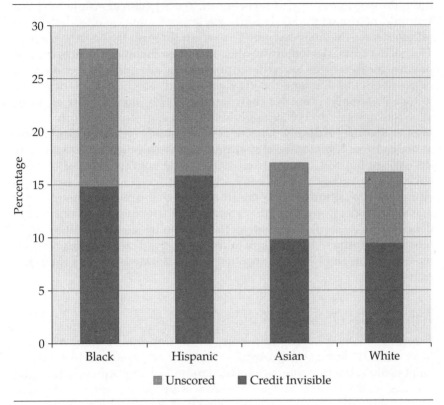

Source: Authors' compilation based on CFPB 2015.

Such insights have encouraged financial institutions to improve their outreach to underserved populations, but they have not addressed more broadly how individuals experience the financial rules and services that place them at such a disadvantage. It is not enough to conclude that the planning-self is willing whereas the acting-self is weak.

What, however, is the alternative? What would it mean to move from inclusion to justice? How can financial inclusion be analyzed as something that happens to a family rather than to an individual obtaining a credit score? What if we were to analyze financial well-being as the respectful management of a bundle of relationships rather than the quantification of liabilities and risks? What would it look like to bear debt with dignity?

Studying the credited, the tenuously credited, and the discredited has long been an obsession among sociologists. Our scholarly community, however, has applied these terms to nonpecuniary situations (for example, race and ethnic relations, gender, and interpersonal dynamics) rather than to the financial world in which these situations are enacted. The sociologists Marion Fourcade and Kieran Healy, who suggest that paying close attention to credit scoring and the allocation of credit would help us better understand the life chances and social identities of people in today's society, point out that, "on the supply side, scoring agencies slice consumers into behaviorally-defined risk groups, and price offerings to them accordingly. On the demand side, consumers find themselves more or less comfortably fitting into these categories—which, by design, are not constructed from standard demographic classifications such as race and gender." Credit scores help create new classification situations, "positions in the credit market that are consequential for one's life chances, and that are associated with distinctive experiences of debt."[4] How do credit scores affect the ways in which people fit together into social groups? How does an individual's good credit score or inability to generate one affect her connections with others (family members or friends)?

THE ORIGIN OF THESE QUESTIONS

These questions of citizenship emerged during our research with the Mission Asset Fund (see prologue). We were attracted to MAF, not for what it could tell us about citizenship, but rather and primarily for what it could reveal about financial inclusion and economic justice. We soon learned the importance of understanding that the personal experiences of MAF clients with debt, credit, and good credit scores extend well beyond the act of obtaining a social loan.

When we conducted our interviews with fifty-seven MAF clients in the summer of 2015, three to four new lending circles were being formed each month at the Mission District office alone, with roughly ten people per circle. Clients took out loans of $300 to $2,400—the average loan being between $500 and $1,000—to be repaid over a ten-month period. Since 2007, the Mission Asset Fund has provided over 9,200 interest-free social loans worth $8.3 million among all participants in the lending circles in over seventeen states and the District of Columbia. The MAF main office also operates as the hub for research and development, fostering conceptual innovations and testing new ideas. Compared to what they would have paid elsewhere, MAF clients save about $360 in fees and interest on each social loan, amounting to a total of $1.6 million in savings. Presumably, these savings in fees and interest help clients reduce their debts and direct their resources toward helping themselves and their families.

At first, we focused on the practical reasons why MAF clients wanted credit scores and a means of building a positive credit history, but we soon noticed that nonmaterial concerns were equally important to them, such as being treated with respect and acting honorably toward family and loved ones. They reckoned that access to a mainstream credit card would signal their arrival at adulthood and stability. With a credit card, they could enter a store and do what others did, or they could enter a bank and be treated like everyone else. We saw above all a longing for equality in the market (if not under the law).

As some MAF clients explained to us, people with bad credit are treated as if they do not know what they are doing. Even financial counselors can sometimes make those without a credit score feel as though they lack the self-control and good judgment to keep themselves out of trouble. There is no recognition that these clients are not necessarily "giving in to temptation," but rather making choices about how to honor requests from loved ones. Often they fall into debt, not for their own sake, but for the good of people whom they care about.

Most of the individuals we interviewed for this book identified social connections as a vital need, and many wished to improve their finances to help not only themselves but others as well. People spoke about assisting their children, parents, siblings, and friends as a way of honoring the right of loved ones to make such claims ("relational rights"). In *Economic Lives*, the sociologist Viviana Zelizer reminds us that we show respect and concern for those we love in the ways we use our resources both with them and for them.[5] How we handle money also signals our closeness to other people and our role in their lives, and theirs in ours.

We found that when dealing with credit and debt, MAF clients were managing more than their relationships. They were trying to participate in an imagined social contract in which honesty and decency generate just rewards, including the feeling of being connected to socially significant others. Interviewed by NerdWallet about his experience with the lending circles, Javier Giron, a forty-six-year-old immigrant entrepreneur, remarked: "Credit is gold in the U.S. [Without it,] you don't have anything." For someone like Javier, credit functions as a capability, what the economist Amartya Sen calls the set of "beings and doings" that lead to self-actualization.[6] Without credit, Javier would not be able to make his own decisions or pursue his dreams. Worse, he would be marked as someone lacking the capacity for judgment—as an adult unworthy of autonomy because his decisions would not be deemed legitimate.

THE FOUR COMPONENTS
OF FINANCIAL CITIZENSHIP

Such stories of credit invisibility and its effects challenge our understanding of citizenship and belonging. We use the term "financial citizenship" to indicate membership in a market-oriented public whose privileges depend on credit scores and external signs of credibility. Having one's financial credibility fully recognized requires a right to safety (freedom from exploitation), a right to recognition and belonging, and a right to become what W. E. B. Du Bois called a co-creator of one's culture.[7] Historically, disadvantaged co-creators appear as "two souls warring in the same body": they experience their financial practices as a means of gaining social belonging, dignity, and respect, but they are also pushed to see their behaviors through the gaze of others. This external gaze too often renders them "Quants," that is, calculating individuals who are more concerned with maximizing material gain than with living a dignified life in a caring community.

Neither the advantaged nor the truly disadvantaged behave like Quants. Analogously, individuals' claims to financial citizenship go beyond the formal meaning of membership in a national community. The definition of financial citizenship that emerges from the ground up differs sharply from depictions of the financial system as necessarily dominating society and those who dwell therein. Writing in the mid-1990s, for example, the economic geographers Andrew Leyshon and Nigel Thrift noted the contradiction between social rights and market freedom. With market freedom, financial citizens can experience discrimination (by price) and both buyers and sellers can take advantage of each other as long as they honor contracts and do not violate laws.[8] How, then, can we speak of citizenship in an environment in which free market principles have emerged as dogmatic tenets of faith?[9] Is it possible, the geographer Mark Kear asks, that banks and other financial institutions have a social contract with customers and noncustomers alike?[10]

In *Citizenship and Social Class* (1949), T. H. Marshall argues that citizenship transcends the formal rights granted by governments and extends to the informal consensus on what people should be able to accomplish if they belong in the society in question. He also points out that different types of citizenship emerged in capitalist England as the democratic impulse clashed with the inequalities inherent in a free market system. The earliest period of civil rights had led to later periods of political rights, then social rights. The more Marshall looked, the more he found a range of rights to which workers had given voice. They wanted a say in how industries were run, for example, and how they were called on to labor in those operations ("industrial rights"). Perhaps less discussed in general were the "consumer rights" that Marshall identified, including "the right to share to the full in the *social heritage* and to live the life of a civilized being according to the *standards prevailing in the society.*"[11]

In short, as people become full members of a financialized society, they assert their freedom *from* and their rights *to*: their freedom *from* exploitation, and their right *to* recognition, social belonging, and the co-creation of institutions of commerce.[12] These components of financial citizenship bear a strong resemblance to what the political theorist Danielle Allen calls political equality, and this resemblance affirms just how embedded society and politics are in the world of household finance. In the rest of this section, we review each of these four components.

Freedom from Exploitation

Consumers expect to pay interest on borrowed money and to incur fines for not paying their bills on time. Although many consumers are exploited on a regular basis, we want to make clear that this is not simply a quantitative problem of high interest rates or exorbitant fees and fines. Certain quantitative benchmarks do elicit public outrage, such as the 300-plus percent annual interest paid on payday loans or the subprime mortgage rates and fee structures that make it harder for disadvantaged families to build equity in their homes. At what point, we may wonder, do banks and other financial providers go too far? What is the line between profit-making and exploiting the needy? And why not consider the alternative explanation that so-called exploited individuals are freely choosing their options?

We recognize that individuals experience situations of explicit exploitation and encounter disadvantages that result from quiet, longer-term processes. Even when obvious, financial exploitation is difficult to correct because it can easily be blamed on the "choices" made by its victims. By contrast, its quieter forms escape the attention of policymakers, who seem confused about how to address historically entrenched disadvantage. The first is easy to illustrate; the second takes time to discern.

In cases of explicit exploitation, the providers of financial services target vulnerable individuals. Take, for example, an individual who has opened a mainstream bank account to avoid check-cashing services, pawnshops, and payday lenders.[13] To her surprise, that bank, extolled by financial counselors, is the problem. Wells Fargo staff have opened accounts under her name to make money off her. Although she realizes that the bank is engaging in fraud, she is convinced that no one will believe her. It is her word against Wells Fargo's. She has neither the time nor the monetary resources to confront the bank; moreover, the bank enjoys legal protection that precludes her and customers like her from joining a class-action lawsuit.

Similarly, it is difficult to confront deception that cannot technically be classified as deception. Financial providers take advantage of widely known patterns of behavior that lead people to accumulate high-priced debt. For example, payday lenders offer loans with balloon payments (as do mortgage lenders in the subprime market). The timing of the balloon payments leads potential borrowers to discount the cost of the loan or overestimate their ability to pay it. The problem in this case is not the fact that consumers have common cognitive inclinations (under-estimating costs and overestimating their ability to keep up with payments); the problem lies in the very design of a loan product that takes advantage of these inclinations with the intention of locking consumers into debilitating debt.

No matter how disciplined or, conversely, out of control a person may be, there are certain exploitative situations that they simply cannot bring on by themselves. Describing the predicament of a forty-seven-year-old woman whom she interviewed for a *New York Times* story, Gretchen Morgenson observes: "As surely as it takes two to tango, [this woman] had partners in her financial demise. In recent years, those partners, including the financial giants Citigroup, Capital One and GE Capital, were collecting interest payments totaling more than 40 percent of her pretax income and thousands more in fees."[14] While acknowledging that the subject made some poor and costly decisions, Morgenson identifies the terms of the interest payments, fees, and fines as the culprit that still walks free. Had the loans this borrower took not been structured in the way that they were, she could not have made her "choice." Her decision had required institutional assistance. The institutions from which she borrowed had been quick to hand her a shovel (of their own design) to dig the trap into which she fell. It did not have to turn out that way.

Other cases of exploitation unfold over far longer periods of time, sometimes without obvious indicators of abuse. In *How the Other Half Banks*, the legal scholar Mehrsa Baradaran shows that African American institutions of commerce have operated with different levels of protection and more limited access to growth opportunities.[15] Even when these institutions have done all the right things, their return on investment has been lower than that of mainstream institutions. Initial conditions of disadvantage shaped the ecosystem in which they and those they support engage in financial transactions. This is a less obvious form of exploitation, as we shall see in chapter 2. To correct the false impression that the wealth gap and over-indebtedness result from ignorant individuals making poor choices, we need to pay attention to processual exploitation. And we need to remember that there are some things that individuals and nonprofit organizations cannot accomplish on their own. Public policies matter.

The Right to Respect

According to José Quiñonez, well-meaning policies may unintentionally create problems simply by treating the people they are trying to help as if they were incapable of making good decisions. According to this premise, if these people could make sound choices, they would need neither assistance nor specially tailored programs. This narrative scours people's experiences for those instances when they seemed to work against their own well-being, as when they took on debts they could not afford, or sent money to relatives rather than contribute to their own retirement funds or their children's educational funds. Such policies determine for these people what their legitimate needs are; tell them that they have no right, as it were, to put their money in the service of those they love; and identify priorities that others do not recognize as such. In short, the right to recognition of the people they would help is denied.

The philosopher Axel Honneth defines the right of recognition as the external acknowledgment that an individual has the capacity to reason and engage in public deliberation on what constitutes a legitimate need.[16] In the case of financial citizenship, an individual receives respect and recognition when public officials and nonprofit practitioners do not denigrate her household budgeting practices, even practices that they deem unwise or wasteful. This right to recognition runs counter to the urge to "fix" broken people. It also requires that those who witness harmful or wasteful financial practices tolerate the individual who is learning from experience and who may simply need greater protection from exploitation and alternative institutions of commerce to meet her legitimate needs. That being said, such tolerance may facilitate the conditions of exploitation. But if intolerance is to be practiced, it should be aimed at the exploiters, not the exploited.

The Earned Income Tax Credit (EITC) is a government program that helps individuals exercise their right of recognition. Low- and moderate-income individuals receive a lump sum of cash and obtain this lump sum using the same facilities as do higher-income taxpayers. Jennifer Sykes, Katrin Križ, Kathryn Edin, and Sara Halpern-Meekin have studied how the EITC affirms the dignity of those who participate in the program by routing them through mainstream service providers, such as H&R Block.[17] When these same individuals receive their government benefits through stigmatized services such as the welfare office, their sense of self changes: they are made to feel that they are not like everyone else and that they are not in fact collecting money they have *earned*. Using H&R Block signals to them that they do have the capacity to reason and the freedom to make choices about how they use their resources. In another study, Edin, along with Luke Shaefer and Laura Tach, goes beyond the EITC to ask: "What if any program, public or private, seeking to help the poor were designed with social inclusion as a defining principle?"[18] In this book, therefore, we define the experience of "social inclusion" and "financial citizenship" as a multifaceted condition that explicitly includes the right to recognition.

Let us first consider how people may experience disrespect. As parents struggle to protect their children from eviction and help them lead normal, fulfilling lives, they find themselves battling collection agencies that not only demand payment but also insist on shaming them. One woman reported that an agent from the United Collection Bureau called her about a nonfederal student loan that was in arrears. He informed her that the front door to her house would be padlocked and that she would be handcuffed by the sheriff. Upon calling the bureau to see what could be done, "the man I spoke to became belligerent and cussed at me. He told me that is why I am in collections because I am a loser. *My daughter heard this as the call was on speaker phone. She started crying and asked why this mean man was calling you a loser, Mommy.*"[19] With her child within earshot, she had experienced her dignity as a mother being jeopardized. Not only was she not able to protect herself, but she had also failed to shield her daughter from the pain of indebtedness. Perhaps worse, if her daughter saw that she could not demand recognition and respect from others, what prospects would her daughter have as an adult?

Such denials of respect and recognition become part of government policy when financial literacy tests become a prerequisite for accessing critical services. Working its way through the legislature in Kentucky, for example, is a bill that would require individuals who receive Medicaid (for needed medical care) to undergo a financial and health literacy examination to get back on the program after being kicked off.[20] The bill is a consequence of the new work requirement, which stops coverage for Medicaid recipients who cannot meet it. The requirement can be waived, however, if an individual passes a set of health and financial literacy quizzes that are allegedly designed to help people make better decisions when selecting health care plans or managing health care expenses. But they also resemble the citizenship tests used in the Jim Crow South to prevent black citizens from voting, while signaling to the individuals required to take them that they cannot afford health insurance on the private market, or that they have "avoidable" ailments. In other words, these new requirements imply that the affected individuals have acted out of either ignorance or a low capacity for making legitimate decisions on their own. These quizzes make it impossible for low-income individuals to stand on the same moral ground as their higher-income insured counterparts. Karl Marx recognized early on the moral dimensions of debt and credit. He wrote: "Credit is the *economic* judgment on the *morality* of a man . . . the *spirit of money* is not money, paper, but instead it is my personal existence . . . my social worth and status."[21] A lack of credit and the weight of debt can threaten both how worthy others regard an individual to be and how that individual regards herself.

The right to respect runs counter to the reluctance of dominators to treat the dominated as moral equals. Adam Smith makes this argument in *The Wealth of Nations* as he discusses slavery in the colonies: "The pride of man makes him love to domineer, and nothing mortifies him so much as to be obliged to condescend to persuade his inferiors."[22] Dominators justify their superior status by noting that the dominated seem to work with less enthusiasm than they do; the oppressed, they assert, lack discipline, as opposed to their own self-regulation and self-control. Moreover, the negative qualities of the dominated have consequences for their health, education, and financial security, which can threaten the well-being of the healthy. Why should the strong be subjected to incoherent or dangerous narratives spun by the weak? What is more, if left unpunished, the behaviors that wreck the lives of the poor may contaminate the morally upright. Such reasoning allows the powerful and the well-meaning to abandon the right of recognition for the sake of protecting the entire community and helping its weak members grow stronger.

Debt collectors justify their disrespectful behavior toward those in severe breach of contract by invoking the dominator's logic. Why treat such individuals with respect? Indeed, the experience of being treated with disrespect by the mainstream financial system may have motivated some individuals to use higher-cost financial services. As at least one MAF client remarked, "When you get money from a pawnshop, it's your own stuff, so they don't ask a bunch of [disrespectful] questions." Pawnshop operators do not treat one's possessions as if they are dirty, contaminated, or contaminating. By the same token, even more vilified sources of short-term loans, such as payday lenders, seem to know how to engage in recognition, even as they practice exploitation. They know that having short-term needs is natural in our financial system and do not look with suspicion at anyone trying to provide for his or her family in a dignified way (as we discuss in greater detail in chapters 3 and 4).

The Right to Belong

What does it mean to belong to a family, a community, or a society? The term "belong" invokes connection. What are the visible indicators of such a tie? What are the implications of social connections for healthy human development? These questions broaden the purpose of financial citizenship beyond the material disadvantages experienced in the marketplace to ask how credit invisibility and stigma become implicated in the way we look for work, perform in school, engage in politics, and participate in community or religious rituals. In other words, if human well-being now depends on membership in a financialized community, how do we think about the right to social belonging with regard to the financial system?

We know that a person belongs to a group and its traditions by virtue of how she uses her financial resources.[23] A family demonstrates that it belongs to a religious or cultural tradition by paying for a bat or bar mitzvah or a quinceañera. Parents and guardians affirm their children's belonging in a school community through visible purchases for their graduation ceremonies and by their willingness to do whatever it takes to help their children pursue a college education or to complete other rites of passage.[24] Parents also help their children feel part of a peer group by allowing them to wear and use the same things as their peers do.[25] Parents see no reason why their children should not enjoy Christmas as other children do and know that, when they return to school after the December holidays, they will feel pressure to reveal what they received for Christmas. If they have received nothing, the children may feel shame, and their parents may feel worthless.

This intrinsic drive for social connection needs to be accomplished in a dignified, affirmative way. First, wrong timing can draw unwelcome attention. Communities undulate with rhythms as its members move in step, fulfilling rituals and traditions. If a member falls out of step, she may draw sharp criticism from others. So, for example, a family needs to celebrate a graduate on graduation day, not at a later moment when they have saved enough income or other lumpy expenses are not interfering. Second, how individuals pay matters. It is not just a question of providing the feast for the graduation party but also of how the parents, or those in the role of parents, visually pay for the event. Do they use a credit card or a gift card, as do other parents in such cases, or do they cook at home after acquiring groceries from governmental or nonprofit sources? Hence, the ridicule in an Eddie Murphy comedy act toward children whose parents cannot afford regular cheese and have to rely on "government cheese." Worse than a stigmatized source of funding is a publicly declined credit card at the checkout. Rejection occurs before loved ones and marks the parent as unable to provide adequately (or plan properly) for an important transition in her child's life.

For too long, proponents of liberty have emphasized freedom *from* belonging rather than the right *to* belong. Too much belonging, in their view, puts restrictions on where individuals can work, what they can sell, and how they can consume by virtue of their gender, race, religion, or social status. Just as Georg Simmel identifies money as the social leveler that did away with unnecessary status distinctions and antiquated requirements to belong to a group, those who believe in mathematical purity turn to credit scoring as a way of freeing the grantors of credit from their own prejudices. An unbiased, mathematically driven market will generate fairness and efficiency so long as historical processes of exploitation can be bracketed. In a financialized society, people no longer need to say that all money is the same color and can now state that all financial histories are simply pure math (universal) in that each has a number. Simple math liberates even those struggling with implicit prejudices, allowing them to make judgments based on the universal characteristics of individuals (work histories, skill sets) rather than on particular, ascribed identities (ethno-racial categories, gender or sexuality, religion, or national origin).

Yet these algorithms and the actions that they facilitate rely on a vision of the world that encourages disconnection, or at least a limited and highly selective connection to family and community. From this perspective, individuals unmoored from their past have an abundance of options. They can choose new families and move away from old ones. They can decide how to earn, what to save, what to borrow, how to invest, and to whom to lend. According to this individualistic view of consumption, the unequal outcomes that result from their choices are necessary. The capacity to choose is intrinsically valuable in and of itself. What matters is equal opportunity that allows disciplined individuals to reap material rewards.

By contrast, we ask in this book how the menu of available choices is established for different groups. We argue that what anyone perceives as an option depends on what others around them are doing. Options operate not globally but locally; thus, if your sibling needs financial help and cosigning a loan or obtaining a payday loan is an option that others in your social circle exercise, it becomes harder to argue that the option should not be on the table. By virtue of being asked to help, you experience social belonging and are marked as tied to and responsible for the well-being of another.

Native Hawaiians offer a clear example of what it means when individuals act as though they are enmeshed in a web of relationships. In a case study of the Hawaiian Community Assets Organization, a community leader placed relationships at the center of financial health: "The Western tool of hoarding dollars and of building financial strength is not the endgame—that is not the reason we seek to build wealth. We build it for the Native endgame: to spend it on and to invest in Native goals, to achieve language revitalization . . . to immerse [our youth] in Native cultural values . . . and to set a foundation for Native Hawaiian wellbeing."[26] This Hawaiian nonprofit, in short, is trying to tailor its programs and services to entire families, enabling individuals to incorporate their offspring and other members of their multigenerational families. For example, they turn budgeting and other financial practices into a family-oriented and participatory activity.

This case study represents what Jessica Santos, Angela Vo, and Meg Lovejoy have termed "empowerment economics." According to their definition, empowerment economics engages in shame-free dialogues with families because it is the group rather than the individual that makes financial decisions. This sort of relational approach leads to multigenerational interventions that are based on culturally resonant terms. Not only does an empowerment approach meet people where they are, but it also does not predetermine where they need to go (goals). In this model, the targeted population has a right to a say in the goals established and the types of interventions that it wishes to experience.

The Right to Co-create Institutions of Commerce

In our observations of lending circles, we noticed that as individuals joined the program, they implicitly affirmed their right to have access to commerce as well as to coproduce and codirect the commercial institutions they used. The loans originated from the group, and the structures (the rules, the platform, the reporting procedures) were put in place to optimize benefits for members. As we shall see in chapter 3, lending circle participants were repeatedly told that members of the circle needed to determine loan amounts and had to figure out what to do if one of them asked to change the month in which she received her lump sum. They were also regularly reminded that they were lending their own money. This experience differed sharply from typical encounters with commercial institutions, which are highly directive, nudging people out of "bad behaviors" with such force as to demean them and depriving them of any sense that what they receive is something that they have co-created and are free to use as they wish.

To assert a right to commerce requires a grounded understanding of what commerce is. Like other social institutions, such as the state and the church, commercial institutions help organize people's lives while offering sanctioned scripts for good versus bad behavior. By doing so, commercial institutions offer both a means of self-expression and self-actualization and a means to connect with socially significant others. Writing in 1913, the sociologist Charles Cooley regarded self-expression as necessary for "self-respect and integrity of character" and saw commercial institutions as potentially engendering such traits.[27] Yet Cooley also acknowledged that people need to believe that they have a stake in a society in which pecuniary values are on the rise and some sort of "control of working conditions by the state or by unions, co-operation, [or] socialism—something that [gives them a sense that they have a] human share in the industrial whole of which [they are members.]"[28] It was "bad philosophy, in economics as in religion," Cooley wrote, to consider material matters like money and finance as unrelated to higher cultural values such as dignity, creativity, and social belonging. "To separate them is to cripple both, and to cripple life itself by cutting off the healthy interchange among its members."[29]

Commerce, after all, signifies the circulation and interchange of a wide variety of things, ideas, people, relationships, and values. Monetary transactions rely on these other transfers. Albert O. Hirschman's depiction of "doux commerce" reminds us that the acts of buying, borrowing, and saving draw people into relationships motivated by interests and passions, that these ongoing interactions in the marketplace smooth out differences (or turn them into motives for connection), and that ongoing interdependencies make us behave more kindly toward one another.[30] In *Economic Lives*, Zelizer also notes that doux commerce is not dead. There is no linear progression from a longing for community to a fierce insistence on being left alone. Instead, people express love, intimacy, and community through their handling of money, and they make sacrifices for loved ones through debts, gifting, and other forms of financial provisioning.[31]

Credit unions, which are co-owned and governed by those who use them, have served as an exemplar of institutions that thrive on social connection. Being owned by its members places limits on how much

Table I.1   The Four Components of Financial Citizenship

Component	Definition	Examples
Right to be free from exploitation	Being protected from deception and coercion	Being protected from hidden fees and balloon payments meant to keep borrowers paying more than advertised on a debt
Right to respect	Being treated as if one's decisions are valid	Not being subjected to financial literacy tests that signal an individual's unfitness to make her own economic decisions; not being asked questions that suggest an individual's disabling lack of financial know-how (even if the evaluator believes the disability to be significant)
Right to belong	Being able to use credit and debt in order to participate in family and community rituals; being able to treat requests from loved ones as valid (relational rights)	An individual not meeting savings and investment goals because of the need to cover expenses that allow her child to participate in an activity, as other children do, or that allow her or those she cares about to participate in a rite of passage
Right to co-create institutions	The freedom to use expertise from both local, unofficial practices and official, nonlocal practices (for example, banks and other formal financial service providers) to make new hybrid products and services	Formalizing rotating savings and credit associations into lending circles so that consumers can build a positive credit history; using the model of funeral societies to develop insurance alternatives that resonate with communities

Source: Authors' compilation based on CFPB 2015.

profit the credit union's management can make and the kinds of penalties and fees that members are willing to accept as necessary for the institution and the community it supports to thrive. Credit unions represent a particular vision of economic democracy. In such a financialized *demos*, service providers strive to be economically healthy while also being connected to those they serve. Table I.1 brings together the right to co-create institutions with the other components of financial citizenship, namely the right to be free from exploitation, the right to respect, and the right to belong.

RECOGNIZING ACCOUNTS

The fight against inequality has expanded to the provision of credit visibility, the recognition of dignity, and the extension of choice. At first glance, these accounts of citizenship seem mismatched, with politics, sociability, and dignity imposed on economic life. With greater care, we hope to demonstrate the usefulness of our alternative account and to make sense of behaviors that might otherwise escape our understanding.

We find our blueprint for thinking through these social accounts of credit, debt, and citizenship in a character in a short story by Jorge Luis Borges. Zelizer retells the story in *The Social Meaning of Money* to elucidate what people do when they account for money and its uses. The character, Ireneo Funes, is incapable of sleep but has a remarkable memory, hence his moniker, Funes the Memorious. When referring to numbers, Funes uses terms that mainstream accountants and regular folk do not recognize:

> Instead of seven thousand thirteen, he said (for instance) *Máximo Perez;* instead of seven thousand fourteen, *The Train;* other numbers were . . . *Sulphur, clubs, whale gas, cauldron, Napoleon, Agustin de Vedia.* Instead of five hundred, he said *nine.* Each word had a particular sign a sort of marker. . . .
> I tried to explain that this rhapsody of disconnected voices was precisely the opposite of a system of enumeration. I told him that to say 365 meant three hundreds, six tens, five ones—an impossible analysis with the "numbers" *Dark Timothy* or *meat blanket.* Funes did not understand or did not want to understand.[32]

Failing to grasp his method, someone casually encountering the bedridden fellow might mistake him for mad. However, trying to force-fit an "ideal of numerical calculability" on Funes would deprive him of his voice. Had he used a conventional term for a number rather than *Dark Timothy*, he would not have been able to convey the cultural, sonic, pictorial, or moral meanings he had in mind. Calculation carries quantities, histories, sound, and sense. In our view, Funes has a right to his creativity.

Like Funes the Memorious, many people have memories of money that, though less complete, transcend its quantitative character. We will meet some of these people in this book and see how they manage to juggle the financial needs of several households with little money and even less formal education. Do such individuals need a completely new system for managing their finances, or does it work to simply amplify what works well while minimizing what does not? It is not math alone that spirals a family down into harmful debt. Math without meaning, we argue, disrespects those who use it to calculate. Worse, it provides a technocratic excuse for depriving people of their citizenship.

Accounting functions as voice. It can silence relationships, moral concerns, and histories of disadvantage, or it can reveal and make these experiences and values integral to the system of enumeration and critical within the practice of repair. The individuals we met at Mission Asset Fund spoke about *why* they had made financial decisions more than *how much* those decisions had cost them in quantitative terms. Through their finances, they gave voice to their aspirations for their children, their insistence on a dignified death for loved ones, their performance as providers and protectors, and their strong desire to be treated with respect as they engaged in transactions to co-create their communities. The meaningful lives they pursued defy top-down instructions on getting a single number "right"— the "right" target for savings or retirement, the "right" kind of place to bank. Policymakers often act as though the nonmathematical language of spending and borrowing can be directly translated into a mathematical bottom line and hard numbers will persuade individuals that one course of action is preferable over another. Such unidimensional translations on the part of policymakers ignore the meanings of money, credit, and debt, often with perilous consequences for those individuals' lives.

AN OUTLINE OF THE BOOK

Chapter 1 opens with the birth of the Mission Asset Fund—how a charge to economically empower the residents of the Mission District in San Francisco resulted in lending circles, a new model for bringing dignity, recognition, and belonging to disadvantaged populations. Here we discuss what it means to be a co-creator of a commercial institution and how the principles of financial citizenship emerged at the organization's founding. We follow José Quiñonez into the halls of Congress as he meets with legislators and practitioners in the asset-building community in order to bring certain populations out of the shadows and into opportunity. As we hear him testify about people whose life chances were significantly improved by credit visibility, we begin to examine the need to update old-fashioned notions of inequality and belonging and to take into account the uneven distribution of good credit scores and visible credit histories across the population. Unseen drivers of inequality, such as credit invisibility and the disrespectful engagement of financial service providers with people of color, have kept the latter separate and unequal. The problem arises partly from policy decisions that allow credit scorers to "see" certain behaviors while ignoring other transactions that might demonstrate the ability of those applying for credit to repay their debts. Government regulators try to protect citizens from debt traps and strive to promote sobriety. Sometimes they blame both those who create instruments of debt and those who use them (and "who should know better," as one regulator remarked at a conference on financial inclusion at the Treasury, "than to spend what they don't have"). When assigning responsibility to the former, they affirm the right to be free from exploitation, but when they call out the latter, they deny individuals their right to recognition.

Chapter 2 takes a different tack by embedding the lending circles model in a broader history of racialized disadvantages. Exploitation has long been with us, but some groups of people have been seen as more deserving of protection from it than others. This chapter takes us to the Civil War and its aftermath, when white politicians sabotaged the efforts of people of color to establish new commercial institutions. Certain politicians and historians of the time argued that the country's financial institutions served as the circulation system of the body politic and that "injecting" people of color into its blood would poison it. Later such warnings no longer referred explicitly to race as a contaminant but rather to particular behaviors; those who behaved badly just happened to be clustered in poorer, racially segregated neighborhoods. Later claims by some people that the subprime crisis was the result of extravagant spending among irresponsible people who did not deserve their houses were based on such a view.

The success achieved by social movements did eventually lead to new institutions of commerce that honored people of color and women, but the ecosystem in which these institutions operated remained different. A set of interconnected organizations reduced the ability of people of color in particular to gain as much from engaging in the same savings and investing behaviors engaged in by white people.

Color-blind "postracial" discussions of economics and fairness rely on partial accounts that mask the very arrangements that perpetuate credit inequality today. Legislative attempts to bring credit justice to ordinary citizens have been one answer to the overarching question of who belongs in the United States and what kinds of rights accompany political membership. Nevertheless, racial struggles continue to animate discussions about money and banking, affecting the kinds of help that people of color receive when they try to amass savings, own homes, and realize economic advancement. Identity matters in the marketplace to this day.

Chapters 3 and 4 navigate between these public issues of racialized disadvantage and the experiences of Mission Asset Fund clients as they try to come out of the shadows of credit invisibility. Here light is shed on the MAF staff's recruitment of new clients in community centers and credit unions and on the clients' interactions with the organization and with each other to form new lending circles. "It's not up to us to tell them what their priorities are or how they should use their loans," Mohan Kanungo, the program coordinator, told us. This sentiment was regularly echoed by other staff members and the executive director. In this setting, the practice of financial citizenship achieves a fine balance between the autonomy of the clients and the costs they incur when coordinating activities that help them do and be who they are. MAF clients are not only improving their credit histories but also making consequential decisions for their relationships with loved ones (and those they struggle to care for). However, as we also show in chapter 4, coming out of the financial shadows does not by itself address all of the other forms of inequality experienced by communities of color. With all these lessons in mind, we ask in our concluding chapter how changes to current policies and programs could enhance the experience of financial citizenship for the disenfranchised.

There are ways to misread this book. First and foremost, acknowledging citizenship rights does not "excuse" the abuses of capitalism or promote consumerism as a substitute for democracy. The chapters here lay bare the racialized history of the marketplace and expose the mechanisms for widening inequality. The book goes beyond inequality as status and asks about how people experience it. Using financial services can be either dignity-affirming or morally degrading. While dignity inheres in individuals and may be seen as an inherent right, people can only realize this right by engaging with others. Our emphasis on dignity-affirming transactions forces us to question some of the approaches that scholars and policymakers have taken to studying household finances.

To write this book, we pored through interviews about their financial (and family) lives with fifty-seven Mission Asset Fund clients. Marlene Orozco, a PhD candidate at Stanford, conducted the lion's share of the interviews in the MAF offices. We asked clients about how their lives were going, what they were happy about, and what they wanted to change. We followed up with a series of questions about how they paid their bills, how they helped or received help from other people, and what financial strategies they used week to week, including debit cards, credit cards, payday loans, rent-to-own, salary advances, advances on tax returns, delayed payments on utilities and rent, assistance from family and friends, and assistance from social and nonprofit services. Aside from the client interviews, we have drawn on insights from MAF staff members, notes from our attendance at staff meetings, and observations over a four-year period of recruitment sessions, lending circle formations, financial education trainings, social gatherings, and meetings on how to make financial education available online. We have also examined the histories of race, inequality, and banking in order to understand the long-term processes through which lasting disadvantages were established and have been maintained. From these histories, our observations, and our interviews, we began to piece together how the private financial troubles of the people we met were linked to larger public issues. One of the book's authors (Wherry) interviewed and spent time with MAF's executive director, both at work and at both of their homes. He also spent time with staff members both during and immediately after their workday. In these conversations, staff members revealed their understanding of MAF's mission, and we began to discern some of the unspoken meanings of their work. This led us to thinking about social citizenship, since MAF clients were clearly concerned about belonging and recognition of their membership in their communities was very important to them. We began to see that these concerns about membership and belonging were expressed at the same time as concerns about respect, dignity, and care for loved ones. We encountered self-actualized individuals using money (and whatever else they could find) to do things for the people they loved.

Our experiences at the Mission Asset Fund convinced us that it is time for a financialized understanding of the social contract. Do citizen-consumers have a right to safety? Do they have rights to autonomy and to being treated fairly? How are these rights enacted in a society where credit and credit scoring are imbricated in the relationships among parents, lovers, lone strivers, neighbors, and children? How do consumers' experiences with credit affect their general feeling toward their community and toward democratic society? With these questions on the social dynamics of credit, debt, and belonging, we begin our inquiry.

Chapter 1 | The Invisible Worth of People with No Credit

For José Quiñonez, the case for credit was clear. It was a Tuesday in September 2013 when he headed to the U.S. House of Representatives to explain the consequences of recognizing what actually makes a person worthy of credit. He arrived on the red-eye from San Francisco and freshened up in the airport bathroom before venturing over to Capitol Hill. At the hearing, he reframed the basis of the debate: "I came with pictures, not graphs, not charts." Flashing images of the clients whose stories he was telling, he insisted that the audience recognize his clients' human right to flourish.

See her, really see her, Quiñonez said to those gathered for the hearing as he held up one picture of a client. She is not invisible. Not now. Her name is Veronica, and she long dreamed of owning her own restaurant. She's a hard worker who managed to move from catering to having her own food truck, serving gorditas, horchata, and posole. She has won awards in Marin County culinary competitions, but she could not make the transition from a food truck to a restaurant without a credit score. She was deemed unworthy of the few lines of credit that would allow her to realize her dream because the creditworthy activities in which she was engaged were invisible to the financial system. "So she came to Mission Asset Fund to try to help her build that credit. Within a year or two, we were able to get her from zero to [over 600]. With that credit score, she was able to start these new lines of credit with suppliers and start her business. Now she has her restaurant in Marin County, and it employs over twenty people."

He showed the audience a picture of Helen, whose immediate goal was not starting a business, buying a car, or even owning a house. All she wanted was a safe, clean apartment where she and her children could rebuild their lives. A single mom who bravely escaped an abusive relationship, Helen started over in a new city with two young children. Even though she had multiple part-time jobs, landlords looked only as far as her modest bank account and her credit report before declaring her unworthy. So Helen and her small children rented rooms in other people's apartments and made hallways into bedrooms. After working with the Mission Asset Fund, Quiñonez proclaimed, "Her credit score went from zero to over 670. And with that, she was able to get an apartment of her own where she and her kids felt safe, where they could build a life."

These and so many others had tried to work toward their goals but been blocked by having a low credit score or no score at all. Paying every month and on time for the electric bill, the telephone bill, and the car note was not quite enough to make them trustworthy in the metrics of Vanguard, Experian, Transunion, and FICO. It was time to change that.

The hearing on the Consumer Access and Inclusion Act was slated for the Rayburn House Office Building, a structure described by the *Washington Post* as "Middle Mussolini, Early Rameses, and Late Nieman-Marcus." That day's hearing focused on building credit scores for people who pay their bills on time but remain invisible to credit card companies, banks, employers, landlords, and other service providers. Like social reformers before them, Quiñonez and the legislation's principal sponsors, Congressmen Keith Ellison (D-MN) and Michael Fitzpatrick (R-PA), understood credit as justice, as a means of escaping invisibility and exploitation. This push for credibility followed in a long line of earlier attempts to achieve credit justice (discussed in detail in the next chapter), such as the hearings sponsored by Senator William Proxmire (D-WI) to promote the Consumer Credit Protection Act of 1968, designed to protect people from exploitation while granting them opportunities to provide for their families and participate in community life. Later, in the early 1970s, the Feminist Federal Credit Union recognized the limits placed on the liberation of women with no access to credit. The National Urban League and other civil rights organizations likewise pushed for banking and credit reforms as mechanisms for social inclusion.[1] All these acts of advocacy shared the belief that an inability to participate fully in banking and credit institutions curtails the core freedoms of all citizens and their loved ones.

"Did you know that there are between 35 and 54 million Americans who are credit-invisibles?" A few threads of gray poked through the auburn goatee of Michael Turner, founder and president of the Policy and Economic Research Council (PERC), indicating that he was a man graduated from youth but not yet fully enrolled in middle age. Addressing the hearing room before the arrival of the bill's cosponsors, Turner explained, in the steady tone favored by moderate policy wonks, that information used by credit scoring companies is easily obtainable and can be used to make better decisions. Turner was advocating for credit access as a mechanism for relieving poverty. In his view, any lack of credit visibility was a market failure that could be resolved through a simple information fix if legislation and regulatory clarity allowed such data to be shared. From time to time he glanced at the door in anticipation of the bill's congressional cosponsors, who were caught up in other meetings on a day when important votes were being cast.

Some of the audience began paying more attention to the door, fidgeting as they imagined the arrival of the featured congressmen. The next speaker, Karen Dynan, a deputy secretary of the treasury, offered scripted remarks. First came an apology for the rigidity of the script and her inability to depart from it; next, some background information on the Office of Consumer Policy at the U.S. Treasury; and finally, an explanation of how technology was being used to aid smart data disclosures. Armed with facts, Dynan too spoke steadily, without much inflection: "As we know, as we're looking at the data space, we're seeing a lot of emergence of nonbank entities engaging in financial products and services, oftentimes with data being a core component of the business practice or the economic model. Smart disclosure is a relatively new term, but it's relevant for today's conversation. It's a term for making data more readily available to consumers and to the public, but really to help consumers make more informed decisions. It also creates more transparency in the marketplace for goods and services."

Dynan went on to explain how technology and data visibility would allow markets to work their magic and used products with GPS as a prime example:

> The release of weather data in the late 1980s from government satellites and ground stations has led to the creation of entire industries of weather mapping tools and other devices that are helping all of us navigate our daily lives and get to places we're trying to go. Similarly, the government release of GPS data—which originally was specifically collected for military purposes—has given rise to a huge number of GPS-powered innovations, including aircraft navigation systems and location-based tasks, which are contributing tens of billions of dollars to the economy every year.

What the government did for weather and travel, she argued, it could now do for financial services.

As Dynan began digging into the weeds on privacy protocols and the efficient transfer of consumer information, the door swung open. Republican congressman Michael Fitzpatrick hobbled toward the panel, one leg slung in a cloth cast resting on a knee-high scooter. His face a bit flushed, he acknowledged the panel and deputy secretary. Congressman Ellison of Minnesota was not far behind. Fitzpatrick began with a no-brainer: "The interesting thing about this bill is we're all winners and no losers. Really. The obvious winners would be the 50 million people we're talking about—struggling families in cities in low- to moderate-income neighborhoods, hardworking individuals who are (some of them) renting their housing, newly out of college or high school or at a trade school. They're paying their bills on time. They're paying their cell phone bills, their utilities, and they're paying to a private landlord. Those positive credit activities are not getting reported anywhere, but God forbid you miss a payment!"

Here was a pro-market solution that was pro-growth and anti-poverty. With swagger in his voice, Congressman Ellison remarked, "For those folks who believe in a managed free market economy such as we have in America, we know that good information is key to efficient market clearances. This [bill] gets better information. It gets better information to people who make risk-based pricing decisions. It's more information. So obviously it's going to be a benefit, and it will benefit the macro economy when we get the consumers able to make purchases they couldn't make before and [create] jobs they [didn't have] before." The only problem, he conceded, was determining how to educate people on why something that seemed too good to be true was worth believing in.

Turner and Quiñonez had faced disbelief in the nonprofit community. What if some consumers were now to become doubly disadvantaged because their late utility payments were amplified as indicators of their actual unreliability? In response, Turner had dispassionately run the numbers to assure skeptics that this would not be the case for most people currently invisible in the financial system. According to PERC, the proposed bill would increase credit approvals for blacks (by an additional 14 percent), for lower-income households earning between $20,000 and $30,000 (by an additional 14 percent), and for households earning between $30,000 and $50,000 (by an additional 10 percent). However, there would also be penalties for those with public bankruptcies or severe late payment histories (over ninety days late).

What Turner did not discuss was whether the disadvantaged would be spatially concentrated or whether they would experience an even deeper sense of alienation in the new credit scoring regime. What would this mean for individuals who deliberately paid their utilities late because they prioritized shelter, food, and transportation to work? Would they now be more harshly penalized for using coping strategies that made sense when costs exceeded their income?

As Quiñonez explained, "We came to support the Consumer Access and Inclusion Act because it builds on what's already there. Same strategy, same idea—building on what's already there and not changing what people are doing and not trying to figure out how to rally people. It's using the information that's already there and is already available and helping them to use that to build their credit history and credit score." Quiñonez was not convinced that we knew enough about the specific types of data that should be available to credit reporting agencies, but he did believe that data that are structured, available, and beneficial for the credit-invisible exist but are not used. In other words, if we know that a person pays her rent on time, why should she not benefit from this payment history simply because she does not have the down payment, financial history, and credit access to pay a mortgage of the same amount as her rent (or less) per month? Unlike utility payments, rent payments are not readily available in a structured data set, in part because landlords and apartment managers need to be willing to report on-time payments (and severe lapses) to credit reporting agencies. Such data could conceivably be gathered in a structured way. Quiñonez believed that people who are capable of making payments on time have a right to improve their lives and their families' lives and to be offered an opportunity to do so.

ORIGINS OF THE MISSION ASSET FUND

As he worked on getting the Mission Asset Fund off the ground, Quiñonez found himself in a community of philanthropists eager to support his efforts. What those efforts would entail, however, was not immediately clear. The Levi Strauss Foundation put out a call for applicants interested in establishing an organization supporting economic empowerment in the Mission District, a traditionally Latinx area in which the Levi Strauss Company had long operated a now-shuttered plant. The foundation's $1 million grant included a "description of the executive director position [that] ran four pages," Quiñonez recalled. "When I first read it, my instinct was that I would [eventually] apply for this job, but that I would be the second executive director, hired after the first one failed to meet the unrealistic expectations outlined in the description."[2] The needs in the District were too great for any one nonprofit to tackle. Quiñonez also sensed that he would be passed over for the position because he and his wife, Jennifer Brooks, had a baby on the way. Merle Lawrence, the senior program officer at the Levi Strauss Foundation who interviewed Quiñonez, recalled how up-front he was about his wife's pregnancy. Daniel Lee, the foundation's executive director, noted that during his second interview Quiñonez "probably stopped some folks in their tracks by underscoring his intention to be part of his first child's entire life. This was a powerful declaration."[3] As Quiñonez himself recollected, "I was going to be a father! I was not going to compromise my new responsibilities as a dad to start up a new organization, working 24/7 away from my family."

Quiñonez did get the job and started in a hurry. To generate aware-ness and attract talent, the organization's website opened before the office did. Nonetheless, within two weeks of signing his contract, Quiñonez had leased an office and furnished it: painter's-white walls, modular desks with light-complexioned wood, dark tangerine desk chairs, and random assembly parts scattered across an unused desk. He carried his laptop in each day but kept a printer on location. His close friend Ross Advincula remembered the one-man show. "He was literally pulling it up by the boot-straps. On the phone with a consultant in India while building the website himself. And while his wife was in the hospital, he would be down in the cafeteria for part of the time with his laptop ready to pop back upstairs at any moment." The office assembled, it was time to get to work.

Quiñonez hired Daniela Salas as chief technology officer. He then assembled a team to survey the landscape of financial providers in the Mission District. They looked up providers in the 94110 zip code and in July 2010 sent mystery shoppers to forty-five stores in the area. These individuals pretended to be restaurant employees with credit scores in the low 600s and earnings of $1,500 per month. Claiming to need loans of $1,000, they inquired into loan amounts, loan terms, fees, and interest.[4] What they found were more payday lenders and high-cost loan providers along Mission Street (the main drag) than Mexican restaurants. In fact, alternative financial service providers outnumbered banks about four-to-one across the zip code.

Quiñonez's initial goal was to demystify borrowing by obtaining the right information. Would consumers be able to save themselves the eco-nomic pain of high interest and fees if they had accurate information? How could the information be made easily accessible to them? The one thing that everyone thinks about on a regular basis, Quiñonez reasoned, is food and grocery shopping. Given the reach of public health campaigns, who had not heard about the need to watch calories, fat, or salt intake? When it came to their physical health, for example, shoppers could read nutrition labels to check for ingredients in foods that might raise their blood pressure too high.

Quiñonez and his team at the Mission Asset Fund thus floated a pro-posal for what would become the Financial Facts Label, which resem-bles the nutrition label used for food. Given that the newly established Consumer Financial Protection Bureau (CFPB) was looking for new ideas, he hoped that this model would gain traction. Instead of asking consum-ers to think differently about loans, this label would offer information in an easily understood format. With a "monthly allowance" of debt in mind, a household with a monthly income of $2,000 could be warned against acquiring over $300 in additional monthly debt payments, and those with a monthly income of $3,000 would know to keep their monthly debt payments under $450. The Financial Facts Label gave recommendations on monthly debt payments for incomes up to $6,000 per month, using a debt-to-income ratio of 15 percent to ensure that a consumer (and her household) remained financially fit (see figure 1.1).

In consultation with other nonprofits, the Mission Asset Fund also developed a financial health checklist with questions such as: "Do the loan company employees treat you with respect?" "Are loan documents translated in your preferred language?" "Is the monthly payment for the loan less than 25 percent of your Monthly Debt Budget?" Quiñonez and his collaborators understood that acquiring a loan has as much to do with self-worth as with monetary cost. Why pay interest and fees to a company that treats you poorly?

Quiñonez's own life story was a lesson in visibility and respect. He knew what it means to lose visibility while trying to maintain a sense of dignity. He also knew that making enough money to survive and be able to support the noble pursuits of obtaining a good education and participating in a community of faith can lead to financial struggles. Early tragedies in life made Quiñonez an entrepreneur by necessity and a social analyst by default. Later, in policy school, he honed his analytical skills in order to better understand not only his own story but the stories of so many others who have been invisible or who have tried to make themselves as small and undetectable as possible because being detectable means being a target.

Quiñonez's father, a respected rancher, was shot dead in Durango, Mexico. Once he was gone, the family's assets were snatched away. Consequently, when his mother was diagnosed with cancer, she had no money to be treated properly and died. By the time Quiñonez was nine, he and his five siblings were on their own. The Ashoka Foundation featured portions of his life story on its website the year he was inducted into the fellowship program: "José and his siblings worked hard to support themselves: José sang in crowded buses while his brother tried to collect contributions from bus riders; they sold newspapers and gorditas (stuffed corn cakes) to passers-by in busy downtown intersections; and made body wash scrubbers from agave fiber, selling them house to house."[5] Eventually they were brought over the Tijuana border by their aunt and uncle—all of them undocumented—in search of a better life.

"You learn fast as an undocumented kid not to draw attention to yourself," Quiñonez later recalled. Undocumented children know not to get into trouble in school and not to report any concerns to the teacher or principal. When something happens, they figure out how to handle it themselves. After a while, they learn how to avoid attention—both positive and negative—and how to forgo the right to recognition.

Figure 1.1   The Financial Facts Label

Payday Loan

Pawn / Collateral

Financial Facts
Loan amount $255
1 payment over 14 days

Average Amount Per Payment

Principal $255   Fees & Interest $45

% of Monthly Debt Budget *

Monthly Payment $300   **67%**

Principal $255

Loan Fees $45

Interest $0

APR 460%   •   Total Fees $45

Interest Rate 0%   •   Total Interest $0

Late Payment $0   •   Total Paid $300

Warning: This loan exceeds the recommended portion of your monthly debt budget.

* Percent of Monthly Debt Budget value is based on the loan payment divided by the recommended consumer debt-to-income ratio of 15 percent, using a $3,000 after-tax monthly income level. Debt budget will vary according to your income level.

Income levels:	$2,000	$3,000	$4,000	$5,000	$6,000
Debt budget:	$300	$450	$600	$750	$900

Numbers rounded to nearest dollar.

Financial Facts
Loan amount $1,000
1 payment over 2 months

Average Amount Per Payment

Principal $1,000   Fees & Interest $75

% of Monthly Debt Budget *

Monthly Payment $1,075   **239%**

Principal $1,000

Loan Fees $75

Interest $0

APR 43%   •   Total Fees $75

Interest Rate 0%   •   Total Interest $0

Late Payment $0   •   Total Paid $1,075

Warning: This loan exceeds the recommended portion of your monthly debt budget.

* Percent of Monthly Debt Budget value is based on the loan payment divided by the recommended consumer debt-to-income ratio of 15 percent, using a $3,000 after-tax monthly income level. Debt budget will vary according to your income level.

Income levels:	$2,000	$3,000	$4,000	$5,000	$6,000
Debt budget:	$300	$450	$600	$750	$900

Numbers rounded to nearest dollar.

Source: Quiñonez, Pacheco, and Orbuch 2010.

It was a while before Quiñonez shared his story. Tara Robinson, the director of communications for MAF, recalled that this had less to do with reticence than with his reluctance to draw attention to himself rather than to the work at hand. "You know, when the *Wall Street Journal* came to interview José about the Dreamers loan program, they had no idea that he himself came here as a young kid across the border with his family.[6] During the amnesty program under Reagan, he started his citizenship process. But most of us in the office didn't even know this." These policy changes were consequential for Quiñonez and his family. They reflected just how closely his private struggles were tied to public issues, and why he wanted to engage in the policy domain.

"You can't live the way I have and hold on to rigid beliefs about money management," Quiñonez explained. Much of the policy world treats financial inclusion as a matter of self-control, a position he rejects. "These are not people overwhelmed by temptations. Many are responsible adults who care about their families and simply don't have enough liquidity to deal with small economic shocks. Those who do build up some savings find themselves cosigning for their undocumented parents or for their siblings who need to purchase a car, open a new account at the utility company, or qualify for a mortgage." To say no to a relative for these kinds of purchases is difficult. Yet dealing with an unexpected expense that is the equivalent of a week's wages or more can feel like an insurmountable challenge. "We have to help people see that their financial situations are not inherent in their character but are largely due to external circumstances that they can manage with a little advice and help."

Quiñonez knew what it was like to experience a credit downgrade while caring for a family member. At one point he had cosigned a mortgage with his sister so that she could qualify for one. Although hardworking and responsible, she was not immune to macroeconomic downturns. After losing her job through no fault of her own, she had difficulty making her mortgage payments on time. It was not long before her personal troubles in the financial system became his.

"This really came to bite me when I was nominated for the Consumer Advisory Board to the Consumer Financial Protection Bureau," Quiñonez recalled. The nomination came as a surprise, and a near-derailment propelled him back to the realities of family and budgeting. Robinson initiated the nomination letter. Dated March 27, 2012, the letter reads: "Five years ago, Mission Asset Fund (MAF) was a vision conceived by community leaders in San Francisco's Mission District to narrow the racial wealth gap by enhancing savings and investment opportunities. Just five years later, MAF is close to organizing $1,000,000 in no-cost peer loans among low-income individuals across 10 counties in California. . . . We trail blaze innovative solutions with big impact."

After sorting through over 1,200 nominations, Richard Cordray's office selected twenty-five individuals to join the Consumer Advisory Board. It was then that Quiñonez received the first call from Cordray, informing him that he was a finalist. Then, during the second call, he was told that he had been tapped to chair the board. At that point, all candidates for the board had to submit to a credit check. Quiñonez and his wife were homeowners who lived well within their means. What could possibly go wrong?

To cosign a loan for a relative is to commit oneself to that person for the life of the loan. An industrious immigrant who had made his way to Princeton on scholarship, Quiñonez felt obliged to help his family in any way he could. Who wouldn't? A number of MAF clients had cosigned car notes, explaining that their mother or brother could not get to work without adequate transportation and had had a good job when purchasing the car. For young immigrants with undocumented parents, however, the situation is more complicated. Sometimes parents will use their child's Social Security number, without their knowledge, to open a phone line or hook up a utility. When money is tight, they may wait for the third and final notice of the utility's shutoff before finding the $200 needed to pay the bill. Sometimes the $200 arrives too late and the credit score gets worse, along with the fees to reopen the account. Such children may start life with a horrendous credit score, thoroughly discredited and truly disadvantaged. Conversely, a more economically successful sibling may feel compelled to help less successful ones. "My mistake," one MAF client noted, "was letting my sister use my credit card." These were not people tempted by big-screen TVs or oversized bling, but members of families helping each other survive and live with dignity.

There was another way to help relatives without cosigning—an option that had not been available when Quiñonez was trying to help his sister, but one that he created in time for the request that came from his niece. As he explained, "When she needed to get her credit score up before buying a house, she came to me. She joined a lending circle. She didn't need for me to cosign. I just needed to help her figure out how to have her good payment history, her good financial practices, recognized by the financial system."

Quiñonez recognized the arc of history that had made the credit score so important for him and his loved ones. Credit reporting agencies have a peculiar history and have not always enjoyed the power they now hold. Knowledge of this history, to which we now turn, might help us alter its effects.

SEEING THRIFT, GUILE, AND FORTUNE

The history of credit reporting agencies has been one of finding and cataloging existing information. Imagine a tailor in the United Kingdom in the early nineteenth century. He gradually notices that more and more of his customers are failing to pay their debts. Discussing the matter with other tailors, he discovers that they are confronting a similar situation. Extending credit to customers had worked well when there were few of them and everyone in the community was well acquainted. As tailors and other tradespeople started regarding nonpayment as a common problem, they began conceiving the need for protection from those who sought credit with no intention (or capacity) to repay.

The Society of Guardians for the Protection of Tradesmen against Swindlers, Sharpers, and other Fraudulent Persons was founded in 1826. The organization, which eventually became known as the Manchester Guardian Society, issued monthly reports on persons who did not pay their debts while taking advantage of gossip that identified swindlers. By 1857, the society had established the position of "data accuracy officer" to ensure that the information it received was reliable.

In the 1850s, similar credit reporting agencies started to emerge in the United States, and by the 1900s they had become more prominent. These included the Merchants' Credit Association (what later became Experian), founded by Jim Chilton in Dallas, Texas. Chilton kept a list of not only those most likely to swindle merchants by not paying their debts, but also those most likely to repay on time or early. Known for his notebooks and postcards, he could tell his clients, "Yes, Mr. X drinks too much, but he can be trusted to pay on time." Like Benjamin Franklin, Chilton knew a man to be industrious by his behavior, such as hammering into the night to make repairs rather than hanging out in pubs.[7] But unlike Franklin, Chilton did not seem to care what people did with their free time so long as they paid their debts on time.

Businesses were also perplexed by the dilemma of determining how to handle formerly reliable customers. The scenario is plainly laid out in a 1919 bulletin of the New York Credit Men's Association:

> So far as the merchant can see, there is no change in the customers' income or fixed expenses. The merchant's consent to carry a balance is readily obtained at first. Later, as the account grows beyond the former figures, due chiefly to an ever-increasing left-over balance, the merchant uneasily wonders what to do. . . . The remedy lies in the merchant's own hands. Don't let a prompt customer get the habit of leaving balances. Talk it over with him. Be tactful, but be firm and insistent.[8]

Merchants were advised to keep better records and to issue special credit reports as soon as they noticed a change in a customer's payment behavior. Thanks to the facts provided by the credit report, businesses could make better and timelier decisions, even for those customers who seemed to have no interest in (or history of) making delinquent payments.

The economic historian Daniel Klein argues that credit reporting agencies replaced gossip with verifiable information and that their activities were a more just way of curtailing the temptation to cheat. Noting Adam Smith's 1763 lecture on "The Influence of Commerce on Manners," Klein reminds us that self-interest rather than ascribed national character has led to defaults and that having more information about a customer's behaviors aligns her interest with that of the merchant. Smith also claimed that national or cultural differences matter little if the close-knit nature (in terms of proximity and frequency of transactions) of merchant-customer communities is taken into consideration.

> Of all the nations in Europe, the Dutch, *the most commercial,* are the most faithful to their word. The English are more so than the Scotch, but much inferior to the Dutch. . . . This is not at all to be imputed to national character, as some pretend; there is no natural reason why an Englishman or a Scotchman should not be as punctual in performing agreements as a Dutchman. It is far more reducible to self-interest, [which] is as deeply implanted in an Englishman as a Dutchman. A dealer is afraid of losing his character, and is scrupulous in observing every engagement. When a person makes perhaps twenty contracts a day, he cannot gain so much by endeavoring to impose on his neighbors, as the very appearance of a cheat would make him lose. When people seldom deal with one another, we find that they are somewhat disposed to cheat, because they can gain more by a smart trick than they can lose by the injury which it does their character.[9]

Adam Smith was offering a sociological explanation: in small, tight-knit communities, gossip can maintain social control, but in societies with many anonymous transactions, price signals alone cannot give merchants all the information they need to estimate the likelihood of repayment. Merchants thus turn to ascribed characteristics (country of origin, creed, and family background, for example) to fill in what is missing. What is more, in a tight-knit community, a merchant can discipline customers for late payments or nonpayments, even if he misjudges them.

A 1922 report in the *New York Times* praised the crackdown by the Clearance Bureau of the Associated Retail Credit Men of New York City on "bad check passers, 'dead beats' and their ilk." We can only imagine how much merchandise the "dead beats" detected by the bureau would have obtained from shops had their applications for accounts been accepted. "Bad check passers" found themselves in Tombs Prison, awaiting judgment and enduring shame. These credit bureaus served the public good "by lessening the bad debt and other losses to stores arising from fraud, and thus helping to keep down the costs of doing business and, incidentally, selling prices." The bureau's collection of derogatory information included "accounts closed by members of the association, accounts turned over to attorneys for collection, reports of domestic troubles and other data having an important bearing on credit extension."[10]

Consumer credit bureaus started as not-for-profit enterprises whose operations permitted "two parties, who may be complete strangers, to trust each other and hence to engage in mutually advantageous exchange."[11] Such operations required a more delicate relational touch. In *Retail Credit*, a textbook from 1942, Norris Brisco and Rudolph Severa compared wholesale or commercial credits with consumer credit applications. "Individuals are easily offended when asked too many questions, or when they learn that an investigation is being made regarding them."[12]

The problems associated with retail credit and other consumer transactions were ripe for solutions. Conrad Hilton, founder of the Hilton Hotel, for example, bought the Carte Blanche Credit Company so that he could issue consumer credit to hotel guests. At the time, the hotel had neither an efficient payment system nor an effective way of identifying which customers were most likely to pay their bills in a timely fashion. Hilton invited an engineer, William Fair, and a mathematician, Earl Isaac, to design and implement a comprehensive billing system for Carte Blanche holders.[13] According to company lore, "when Earl Isaac arrived at the [Hilton], he opened a closet and found a pile of mail sacks full of payments that no one knew what to do with."[14] Carte Blanche accepted a lower share of each credit transaction (4 percent) than did either Diner's or American Express, but the company could not manage to stem its losses.[15]

In the 1950s, Bill Fair and Earl Isaac worked out an arrangement with Standard Oil Company of California (now known as Chevron) to gain access to the company's computing mainframe during off-peak hours.[16] Using a supercomputer, the company began increasing the power of its scorecard. Ironically, Standard Oil (which had been owned by John D. Rockefeller in the 1800s) created the Union Tank Line Company, which later became TransUnion, another credit reporting bureau. (In 1981, the Union Tank Car Company sold TransUnion to a company owned by the Pritzkers of Chicago, who today own the Hyatt, Ticketmaster, Nabisco, Colson Associates, and the Pritzker Family Children's Zoo in Chicago.)

A third credit reporting agency, Equifax, was founded in Chattanooga, Tennessee, by the Woolford brothers, Cator and Guy. Just as the Union

Tank Line Company had begun by keeping tabs on customers leasing and buying its oil tank cars, the Woolfords needed to keep up with the payment behaviors of their grocery store customers. In 1901, they founded the Retail Credit Company, which automated its files in 1971 after the passage of the Fair Credit Reporting Act of 1970. When it began trading on the New York Stock Exchange in 1971, the company changed its name to Equifax. In 1994, it joined with the Asociación Nacional de Entidades de Financiaciòn (ASNEF) to expand its linguistic reach.

These credit reporting agencies emerged just as consumer credit scoring was becoming more standardized. Earlier, in 1958, Fair, Isaac and Company had hired Earl Follet to help develop a new scorecard for ascertaining what consumers were likely to do in the future. The scorecard required only a few bits of information: income, bank account balance, outstanding credit, payment history, and time with present employer.[17] The simpler the scoring system, the more likely it was to be used widely enough to increase its predictive power.

In 1970, over a decade later, Fair, Isaac finally managed to sell its credit scoring system to a credit card division of a bank. By 1989, the company had developed its first general-purpose FICO score. As Larry Rosenberger and John Nash note in their survey on the history of information analytics, "Another big breakthrough for the credit industry came when Fair Isaac installed its first general-purpose credit bureau scorecards at Equifax, one of the three major credit bureaus in the United States. With these scorecards, any lender could now measure the credit risk of an applicant or current customer at a cost of just pennies per transaction."[18] By providing a low-cost solution, Fair, Isaac enabled consumer credit cards to take off.

And take off they did. Only 6 percent of U.S. households had credit card debt in 1970; by 2000, that figure had grown to 40 percent. Data and the possibility of quickly processing it had make credit more fair and repayments more predictable. Nevertheless, as the mathematician Kurt Gödel remarked, "Mathematics is perfect, but it is not complete."[19]

PERFECTING CALCULATIONS, LIBERATING CREDIT

What we do with math depends on what the rules allow. Calculations may tell us that one set of loan terms will cost less than another, but the rules may keep us from producing or accessing the cheaper loan. Imagine the following scenario: You are a regulator in Washington, D.C., and you know that existing regulations allow people to obtain a short-term loan from a lender, including a payday lender. Although payday loans last two weeks, most people have to keep renewing the loan. If the individual needs five months to pay back the loan, she will incur about $450 in additional interest and fees on a loan of $300. However, if the regulations were different, it would be easier for banks and credit unions to compete with payday lenders. A borrower could access the same $300 loan with only $75 in additional interest and fees. If you didn't know that the alternative is a payday loan and you only knew the consumer could reduce interest and fees from $450 to $75, would you approve a rule change?

It would seem that paying $75 is better than paying $450 for a loan of $300, but this is not necessarily how regulators see it. They regard lenders as morally suspect and borrowers as irresponsible. If they did not know who the lenders and borrowers were and simply looked at the deal, they would probably agree that paying less is better than paying more. But they are not simply regulating prices; they are also legislating morality.

"If they can't afford it, they don't need it," one regulator remarked. It does not seem to matter to those making this assumption that someone with urgent bills has to borrow money from somewhere, regardless of whether the terms are affordable. In this view, debtors need to learn hard lessons about the wages of sin. Envy that has led them to spend beyond their means, the logic goes, is now inflicting economic pain. In time, the more sensible ones among them will learn their lesson. They will go and sin no more.

Researchers at the Pew Charitable Trusts have asked what would happen if we simply rewrote the rules. What if the problem lies more with those providing the loans than with those accepting them? The Colorado legislature has begun regulating payday lenders by targeting those aspects of the loan that seem to get borrowers into trouble: the big balloon payments, the interest rates, the length of time to repay, and the percentage of the borrower's monthly income that the loan may demand. Once the balloon payment at the end of a loan was eliminated and that payment spread out over five or more months instead, and monthly loan payments were capped at a small percentage of the borrower's income, consumers in the state began paying far less for their short-term loans and became less likely to default on them. The onus of behavioral change was placed squarely on payday lenders. Nearly half of them closed up shop, but those that remained saw their loan volume nearly double. The payday lenders were inefficient, and because of the rule that had governed their operations for so long, they had passed on those inefficiencies (along with predation) to borrowers.

"Here in California," Quiñonez told us, "we are not just going to wait for changes in how payday lenders operate. We're going to increase the competition [among] these short-term loan providers." To do so is difficult because nonprofits, credit unions, and for-profit banks must change how they interact with both regulatory bodies and their customers. For credit unions, stiffer competition would come from both above (the big banks) and below (the nonprofits). A first step, Quiñonez and others reasoned, could be a carve-out: a loan small enough not to invade too much of the incumbents' turf.

On a Thursday in January 2014, California state senator Lou Correa mounted a podium flanked by Quiñonez and Alicia Villanueva. Villanueva, a tamales vendor, had gone from struggling to find money for basic equipment to supplying Whole Foods through her now-profitable venture. With moist eyes, she recalled her early days, when she brought home $200 a week despite working more than full-time, always with her eight-year-old son in tow. For a long time, Villanueva, unable to pay off her debts, could not get financing to invest in her food cart. She knew why: "Nobody trusts you when you have too much debt and a bad credit score, even though you want to work and do better." Her participation in the MAF lending circles had changed that. She now employed seven people and was continuing to work toward fulfilling her dreams.

Reflecting on the lessons he had learned as chair of the Senate Banking Committee, Correa noted, "Sometimes people make it more complicated than it is." And such complications get in the way of generating value. Correa was proposing SB 896, a new section of California's finance code that would exempt nonprofit organizations that offered small zero-interest loans between $250 and $2,500. These are the loan levels that can tip the scale, leading individuals either to slip more deeply into debt or to climb more quickly out of it. Without such a regulation, the cost of social lending can become prohibitively expensive, while the regulatory ambiguity of providing such loans can discourage nonprofits from meeting the pent-up demands of people wishing to enter the financial mainstream. The legislation passed before 2014 came to a close.

CONCLUSION

"You use a credit card when you have to act like an adult. Otherwise, there is so much you can't do," said one of the people we interviewed for this study, describing his situation.[20] Another remarked, "It's as if you're standing right there but no one sees you." Many confessed to feeling invisible, "in the shadows," unworthy to participate in social life the way other adults did. Their invisibility and sense of unworthiness did not stem from any personal lack of a strong work ethic or an inability to be trusted with credit cards and other instruments reserved for adults. Rather, their creditworthy behaviors were simply being systematically ignored. "I mean, I pay my cable bill, my cell phone, my rent," another complained. "I pay on things, and they still say I don't have a credit record." Our interviewees also paid into rotating savings and credit associations and informal funeral societies, often regularly. Why are such recordable events not recorded? Like Ralph Ellison's *The Invisible Man,* those without credit scores are invisible because we refuse to see them.

"Giving credit where credit is due" has become a popular slogan among advocates for financial inclusion. They insist that low- and moderate-income adults are not asking for government welfare, but rather wish to use the free market to improve their lives. They are prevented from doing so by information failures that have kept lenders from seeing whether they are, in fact, worthy of credit even if they have no access to it. Whereas earlier political battles presented banks as unjustly denying loans, in the worst case, or charging too much for them, in the more benign case, these new pleas present banks in a more sympathetic light. Of course banks and credit card companies would like to provide loans and extend services to people who qualify, so long as doing so would allow these institutions to make at least some profit. And technology can now grant individuals a history stripped of race, gender, and religion. All that matters, it would seem, is objective evidence that an individual can make reliable payments on a loan or a credit card bill.

When William Fair and Earl Isaac found data lying around in random piles of paper at Carte Blanche, they used the technologies available to them to look for sensible indicators of people's future financial behavior in order to generate FICO scores. One wonders what they would have done with today's computational techniques. Based on the information before them, would they have found unexpected indicators of a propensity to repay a loan? This is the kind of question that motivated Quiñonez and his team to think about credit-related behaviors that might not have been noticed yet. Because standard approaches had overlooked the practices and priorities of those they wished to serve, they decided to promote a new way of thinking about financial inclusion. Their clients did not need merely a bank account or low-cost financial services; they needed a way to participate in their communities and support and care for their loved ones. Quiñonez knew what many policymakers either did not realize or did not prioritize: that maintaining their dignity and being treated with respect matter to all families making financial decisions, even those living in low-income households.

Chapter 2 | Giving Brown People Credit: Racialized Histories of Money, Credit, and Disadvantage

"GIVING CREDIT WHERE credit is due" requires consensus on who deserves it and why. Should credit, like political freedom, be a fundamental right for all adults? Or is credit a privilege best granted to those who have demonstrated themselves fit to use it, or at least disciplined enough not to abuse it? Such questions animate the issue of financial citizenship. Yet asking them without attention to the history of credit is like letting a book fall open to a page on which the villains stand poised to win: to witness the potential of the underdog, we not only need to read ahead several chapters but also should go back and fill in the earlier part of the story.

Quiñonez had confronted this ahistorical stance in opponents and allies. Any new questions regarding credit could quickly unfold into the binaries of having or not having a bank account, using or not using high-priced financial services, and knowing or not knowing how to use credit safely. Traditionally, such individual-oriented narratives directed the energies of the policy community toward the behaviors of consumers with no regard for their social history. Too often credit regulations focused on individuals' explanations of their past mistakes rather than the role of the very institutions whose rules and practices led these individuals into disadvantage and kept them mired there.

This insistence on equal opportunities only for the financially disciplined has promoted what the marketing expert Tom Burrell calls the "paradox of progress" in *Brainwashed: Challenging the Myth of Black Inferiority*. The myth of a postracial society portrays the racial wealth gap as a consequence of decisions made freely and autonomously by individuals who happen to be people of color. As Burrell cautions, belief in that myth "weakens the impulse to understand or help those still scorched at the bottom of

39

America's melting pot. It fuels the perception that all is well and 'racism is dead,' and suggests that those still wallowing in poverty made conscious choices to live in that stratum. If not . . . they'd simply . . . grab those bootstraps, and go to work!"[1]

Exposing the myth for what it is, a group of economists have been gathering evidence to determine how much grit and determination lie in communities of color. As the stratification economists Yunju Nam, Derrick Hamilton, William Darity Jr., and Anne Price argue in "Bootstraps Are for Black Kids," black and Latinx parents are eager to support their children. In fact, the black parents in their study placed such high value on education that they were willing to help their kids financially through school far sooner than were their white counterparts. For example, they were prepared to do so with assets of $24,887 as compared to the $167,935 that white parents needed before offering similar levels of assistance. These figures are especially alarming when we consider that the rate of return for education is higher for whites than it is for blacks or Latinx, for whom subtle forms of racism, job channeling, and performance evaluations tinged with racial unease offer additional pathways for dampening returns on education. Moreover, unlike black students, white students tend to select majors (such as finance and business-oriented fields), social connections, and job-hunting experiences that lead to higher incomes, all other things being equal.[2] What do all these differences add up to? Blacks and Latinx with education and jobs comparable to those of their white counterparts have less money to save or invest. As Thomas Shapiro notes in *Toxic Inequality*, the processes generating these wealth gaps are toxic in that they damage home, school, and community life while cutting off opportunities for future advancement.[3]

The myth of the postracial society ignores these trends, enabling both policymakers and the public to justify not helping—or even punishing—those most in need of empowerment.[4] According to its logic, when brown people lack discipline and sobriety or have a tendency to shun common sense, they have clearly chosen such paths to low wealth and weak credit scores. Worse yet, if people of color were allowed into the mainstream financial system, they would contaminate it. The one-drop rule has thus been applied not only to intermarriage but also to the comingling of money owned by whites and the presumed "lesser" races. With such sentiments prevailing, policymakers have not been pushed by public opinion to protect people of color from exploitation. Instead, in the racialized history of banking and credit, people of color have been routinely blamed for disadvantages they did not create. In addition, policymakers and financial institutions have not recognized people of color as engaged in positive financial activities, such as fraternal, mutual aid, and funeral societies or the rotating savings and credit associations that serve as models for lending circles. Although people of color do have a history of creating new economic institutions and blending different traditions in order to thrive in difficult circumstances, they have received no credit for their efforts—and all the more so when those efforts have been spontaneous, contingent practices going by various informal names. Worse, their institutions and practices have had to operate at a social discount, unable to realize the full return on the investments that people of color made in them because those same people were already discredited by a racialized rhetoric of inferior worth.

The processes of disadvantage build slowly, sometimes beginning with obvious categorical exclusions based on race and gender. Once foundational inequalities set in, however, even so-called color-blind practices continue widening existing disadvantages. This chapter begins in the middle of the story—with the civil rights movement—and works its way backwards to the foundations of disadvantage in the 1800s. It ends with the present world, in which the Mission Asset Fund and others have been struggling to bring justice to credit.

CREDIT JUSTICE

The civil rights movement was about giving people of color moral, political, and economic credit. In the speech in which he spoke of having "a dream," civil rights leader Dr. Martin Luther King Jr. captured the currency of race and the institutional arrangements that led to inequalities. He likened the rights of citizenship to the practices of banking, arguing that people of color in America were issued checks that bounced *by design*.

> In a sense we've come to our nation's capital *to cash a check*. When the architects of our republic wrote the magnificent words of the Constitution and the Declaration of Independence, *they were signing a promissory note* to which every American was to fall heir. This note was a promise that all men—yes, black men as well as white men—would be guaranteed the unalienable rights of life, liberty and the pursuit of happiness. It is obvious today that *America has defaulted on this promissory note* insofar as her citizens of color are concerned. Instead of honoring this sacred obligation, *America has given the Negro people a bad check; a check which has come back marked "insufficient funds."*[5]

Although King did not mean to replace racial justice with justice focused solely on credit, his metaphor centers our understanding of justice on the economic transactions of ordinary people. The freedoms that come with citizenship, King recognized, would be made manifest by the opportunity to participate meaningfully in the economy. After all, "what does it profit a man to be able to eat at the swankest integrated restaurant when he doesn't even earn enough money to take his wife out to dine?"[6] Such freedoms were evident in people's ability to make their own decisions in the pursuit of happiness. King and others realized that these types of pursuits relied on access to core banking and financial services as well as true equality under the law. Yet, as promissory notes were signed, checks cashed, and funds dispersed, people of color were left holding a coin with restricted circulation, or no coin at all.

After the King-led March on Washington for Jobs and Freedom in 1963 came the 1968 Poor People's Campaign. The Chicano activists Rodolfo "Corky" Gonzales and Reies López Tijerina met with King in Atlanta. As chairman of the Chicano organization Crusade for Justice, Gonzales articulated what he wanted the movement to do after the campaign concluded in Washington, D.C. Ernesto Vigil, a member of the Crusade for Justice, cataloged the next steps, noting that "Gonzales focused on issues like land grants, economics ('Industries which come into the Southwest should use human resources available there, rather than place our people in the bondage of welfare by bringing in outside labor'), and cultural rights ('The continued ignoring of our cultural rights has resulted in the psychological destruction of our youngsters')."[7] At the foundations of justice lay the necessity of owning and building assets as well as coproducing and honoring culture.[8]

The government, unfortunately, played a central role in denying access to these opportunities, not only by what it did but by what it failed to do. An abstemious Wisconsin maverick, Senator William Proxmire, wanted to expose these sins of omission and commission by addressing credit justice. He believed that banks were duping American citizens by providing them with deceptive information about the terms of their loans. Why not make credit information as transparent as a food label? Fat, cholesterol, and other culprits were identified and quantified on food labels. Harmful ingredients in loan products, however, could hide in plain sight.

The senator eventually won over a powerful ally in his quest. President Lyndon B. Johnson signed into law the Consumer Credit Protection Act in the East Room of the White House on May 29, 1968, declaring:

> Today is a day that most Americans have been waiting for for 8 long years. With this bill, the Consumer Credit Protection Act, we are entering a new era of honesty in the marketplace.
>
> At long last the consumer will receive the treatment he deserves when he borrows money. The buyer will be allowed to know what the seller has always known—that is, how much interest he will have to pay on a credit purchase . . .

We know that our consumers should be able to shop for credit as knowledgeably as they shop for groceries or merchandise.

When our parents have to borrow for their children's education or to pay medical bills, they should be told not just how much a month they will be paying, but the total debt that they are pledging themselves to sign up for.

When a housewife opens a charge account at a department store, she will not have to compute how much 1½ percent a month comes to. She will be told that the annual rate is 18 percent, and exactly how much of her total bill goes to finance charges.

When a man takes out a personal loan to pay for a new car, the finance company won't be able to say simply "five dollars down and twenty-five dollars a month." The buyer must be told how many months he will be paying, how much of his money pays interest and other carrying charges.

If a man falls into debt, he will not be punished by unreasonable garnishment of his salary. He will not be deprived of food for his family or money for his rent. He will not be fired out of hand.

If a householder or a small businessman falls prey to loan sharks, his body and his property will be protected from extortionists by stiff Federal penalties.

As President, I know of no single piece of legislation which is of more pressing or more personal concern to more of our consumers than this bill. This bill is truly a triumph for truth.[9]

That same day Johnson announced the establishment of the National Commission on Consumer Finance. The president had great hopes for transparency, access, and justice. Had his vision been realized, the floodgates of justice would have opened and the advocates of consumer justice would have come pouring out.

In certain parts of the country, economic justice had a language problem. At the state level, some legislators wanted to ensure that banks delivered information about loans in language that debtors could understand. In 1973, California state assemblyman Richard Alatorre succeeded in passing Assembly Bill 212 to protect consumers who needed or wanted to receive financial information on loan disclosures in Spanish. (Then-governor Ronald Reagan initially vetoed it.) If a merchant advertised in Spanish, that merchant had to make a Spanish-language version of the loan terms available to any consumer who asked for one. If a consumer could be drawn to a car dealership by a billboard or mailing in Spanish, that consumer could reasonably expect the dealership to ensure that he or she was providing informed consent to the contractual terms extended by the dealer. The same logic applied to mortgage lenders and other service providers that targeted Latinx.

The legal scholar Jo Carrillo notes that Governor Reagan justified his veto of the bill by arguing that "a significant number of television, radio, newspapers and other businesses would be forced by financial considerations to eliminate their Spanish-language advertising in the Spanish-language media." He then urged the legislature to take action to create legislation that would protect institutions that were important to the Spanish-speaking community, while ensuring a fair and equitable marketplace.[10] Later that year, the California Civil Code section 1632 was passed with similar requirements, though it did not cover mortgages or home equity loans.

As people of color demanded credit justice, so too did women's groups. As the sociologist Monica Prasad relates, Arline Lotman, who served as the executive director of the Pennsylvania Commission on the Status of Women, argued that credit justice was also an acute problem for women. Wives who managed to obtain a separation or divorce, for example, soon learned that not having a credit history made it more difficult for them to live a dignified life. According to Lotman,

> Denial of credit is not a one-time action. . . . In our credit-oriented economy, it determines where and how a person lives, what kind of home she lives in, whether she owns a car or can obtain a loan to send her children to college. . . . These practices cause a double hardship on minority women. Denying credit because of marital status, sharply limits the ability of the minority woman who is a head of a household—and that includes 57 percent of minority women—to provide for her dependents.[11]

Even women who managed to build a credit history found that it was expunged when they got married or divorced.[12]

Like the law, credit was becoming a social goal and civil right to which all persons deserved equal access. Just as financial institutions portrayed people of color as incompetent consumers, so too they cast women in the role of unwitting spenders. Prasad recounts, for example, that "one credit union manager complained that women would buy furniture, get married, and then quit payment; but when asked 'how many such losses his credit union suffered in the past five years,' he could think of only three or four out of several hundred, a remarkably low default rate."[13] Lenders like this credit union manager did not need evidence, since they had compelling narratives to assist them in their decision-making. Through these narratives, they would identify entire categories of people who did not know how to spend their money, manage their priorities, or function as reliable bank customers.

Before the passage of the Equal Credit Opportunity Act in 1974, a woman needed a man to cosign her application for a loan, regardless of her income and even if she was a widow. As Robert J. Cole reported in a 1977 *New York Times* op-ed, Thomas Taylor, the U.S. Treasury Department's associate deputy comptroller of the currency in charge of consumer affairs, told the Senate Banking Committee the previous summer that he had come to believe that there was "substantially greater noncompliance with consumer credit protection laws than we had previously thought." For example, banks seemed to be selective when disclosing to women the information they needed to provide in order to obtain a loan, recognizing that if a woman wanted a loan badly enough, she would answer "voluntary" questions. Cole noted that "banks might ask for a husband's signature when, under the law, only the wife's was needed. A bank might ask for information on alimony or child support . . . but fail to disclose (as required) that the applicant did not have to answer unless she wanted to answer."[14] Despite advances made in the 1960s and amendments to the Equal Credit Act in the 1970s, women and people of color remained suspect; even credit unions could find ways to discriminate against them.

A CONTAMINATED COMMUNITY, A CORRUPTED SYSTEM

It should come as no surprise that Comptroller of the Currency Thomas J. Curry portrayed the Community Reinvestment Act (CRA) as a social justice tool for protecting people in low-income and communities of color. In his remarks to the National Community Reinvestment Coalition in 2013, he portrayed credit justice as part of an ongoing civil rights struggle. "Dorothy Height, a local civil rights activist, lived a life devoted to improving the community," he told the coalition. "She noted that community service is as important to the giver as the recipient. Serving one's community, she said, is 'the way in which we ourselves grow and develop.'"[15] By ensuring that small businesses and community development projects had bank financing, the CRA could help clean up the stain left by a history of segregation and systemic discrimination.

The sociologist Greta Krippner describes the early events of the community reinvestment movement in 1971. A bank in Chicago had denied a mortgage and a business loan to a Polish person and a Puerto Rican, respectively. The neighborhood association investigated and confirmed that both loans had been denied on the basis of the applicant's location; each lived in a neighborhood undergoing racial transition.

An ex-minister named Shel Trapp rallied forty neighborhood residents on a Saturday morning to engage in financial disobedience. Krippner writes:

> Community residents entered the bank and formed a line, each person taking out $1 in pennies and then immediately re-depositing 50¢, before taking his or her place at the back of the line. The protest went on for hours, seemingly without reaction from bank officials who looked on as tellers mindlessly completed each request. . . . Suddenly, unprompted, an elderly Polish woman named Josephine Kozial took her handful of pennies and threw them to the floor where they scattered in every direction, echoing loudly through the lobby. "Shit!" Bank officials . . . scrambled to collect the pennies and return them to Mrs. Kozial. Now others were doing the same, creating a deafening clamor.[16]

The bank president entered the lobby to calm the protesters. The bank later agreed to establish a community board to review loan denials, and it also made a sizable contribution to the neighborhood association. The bank account holders had asserted their rights to freely assemble and make their demands on the bank. This was financial citizenship in action.

The tie between local social movements and socially engaged lending unraveled before it could be secured. By the financial crisis of 2007, the individuals most disadvantaged within the financial system had become its scapegoats. Accusations flew, most pointing at the Community Reinvestment Act. If a bank or a thrift was federally insured, it had to meet the needs of the community in which it had been chartered, even if that community was low-income, rural, or a community of color. Howard Husock, author of *America's Trillion-Dollar Housing Mistake,* lamented that the CRA had provided perverse incentives for banks to lend to people who were unqualified for mortgages. He referred to a letter to *American Banker,* a financial-sector trade journal, from a compliance officer at a New Jersey bank who claimed that "loans were originated simply for the purpose of earning CRA recognition and the supporting CRA scoring credit. . . . In effect, a lender placed CRA scoring credit and irresponsible mortgage lending ahead of safe and sound underwriting."[17] In the compliance officer's view, letting in unqualified people of color had contaminated the entire financial system and brought it to its knees.

Political pundits actively promoted the image of a well-meaning, politically correct government trying to help people of color by putting the entire financial system at risk. On *Fox News,* for example, commentator Monica Crowley and the finance expert Eric Bolling had the following exchange:

MONICA CROWLEY: Look, if they had any fundamental understanding about what caused the financial crisis, they would be protesting the Democrat Party. Why? You go all the way back to the Community Reinvestment Act, under Jimmy Carter, expanded under Bill and Hillary Clinton—they put the guns to the banks' heads, and said, "You have got to do these subprime loans."

ERIC BOLLING: All right.

MONICA CROWLEY: And so on.

ERIC BOLLING: All right.

MONICA CROWLEY: That's what caused this mess. Protest them.[18]

"There's only one problem with this story," wrote Michael Barr and Gene Sperling. "It isn't true." Senior fellows at the Center for American Progress, Barr and Sperling had both looked at the data indicating that in the 1990s prime—not subprime—lending had steadily increased in low- and moderate-income communities, especially communities of color. It was only in 2003 that President George W. Bush's chief regulator of thrifts, "holding a chainsaw in his hands as a prop[,] boasted of his plans to cut banking regulations, including the scope of the reinvestment act and his enforcement staff, which he carried out over the next two years."[19] The act now covered fewer financial institutions in these communities. Subprime lending soared.

In the public imagination, brown borrowers looked far more menacing than they actually were. If these were the people getting loans that they did not deserve—so the logic went—it was no surprise that the loans went into default and the country along with it. Yet 60 percent of the problematic lending was extended to middle- and higher-income individuals and neighborhoods, which the CRA did not target. And the 20 percent of the subprime loans held by low- and moderate-income individuals had come from institutions not covered by the CRA.[20] Nonetheless, the specter of the presumed incompetence of people of color enabled pundits to interpret the crisis as a low-class and racial contagion. No doubt, some such interpretations were made innocently as fragments of information immediately confirmed long-held narratives about brown people and their relationship to finance.

On February 13, 2008, Sandra Braunstein testified before the U.S. House Committee on Financial Services. As director of the Division of Consumer and Community Affairs for the Federal Reserve, she needed to inform the committee that entire categories of people had been recently shut out of the banking system even when they were creditworthy, and that changes in the financial industry (rather than the behaviors of people of color) had subverted some of the goals of financial inclusion. Addressing the committee, chaired by Congressman Barney Frank (D-MA), she observed: "The debate surrounding the passage of the CRA was contentious, with critics charging that the law would distort credit markets, create unnecessary regulatory burden, lead to unsound lending, and cause the governmental agencies charged with implementing the law to allocate credit. Partly in response to these concerns, the act adopted by Congress included little prescriptive detail."[21] The number of banks and thrifts subject to the CRA, however, had dropped precipitously—by 51 percent—since 1979. How? Mergers and acquisitions had decreased the number of banks subject to the legislation by 10,470.

With changes in technology, the legislation aimed at brick-and-mortar banks had become ill fitted to the digital age. As Braunstein argued, "Credit scoring has provided a mechanism for realizing loan-processing and production efficiencies, and engaging in systematic risk-based pricing. Similarly, the Internet has enabled the collection of deposits and the disbursement of loans from and to virtually any location."[22]

About a month after Braunstein's testimony, Janet Yellen addressed the wild speculations that the CRA was to blame for the financial crisis. President of the San Francisco Federal Reserve Bank at the time, Yellen saw that accusations blaming the CRA and the low-income families it had helped before the financial crisis were still flying about in the media; she responded by clarifying the situation:

> There has been a tendency to conflate the current problems in the subprime market with CRA-motivated lending, or with lending to low-income families in general. I believe it is very important to make a distinction between the two. Most of the loans made by depository institutions examined under the CRA have not been higher-priced loans, and studies have shown that the CRA has increased the volume of responsible lending to low- and moderate-income households. We should not view the current foreclosure trends as justification to abandon the goal of expanding access to credit among low-income households, since access to credit, and the subsequent ability to buy a home, remains one of the most important mechanisms we have to help low-income families build wealth over the long term.[23]

Both Ben Bernanke, chairman of the Fed, and academic research studies upheld the claim that the CRA was not at the root of the financial crisis, but the unfounded allegations enjoyed the support of "common sense."

The suspected culprits were widely known for living well beyond their means and for generating externalities on the budgets of others. Of course those kinds of people were still unfit for this kind of thing.

CONTAMINATED MONEY, UNFIT PEOPLE

Social theorists once praised money for wiping away the distinctions that kept people from engaging as equals. Money does not care about nation, race, or creed, they believed: money is just money. Salvation lies in math because numbers are color-blind. In this view, people can place their hope for equity and social justice in money and the rational institutions that produce and distribute it.

Such theoretical beliefs seem to have been easily suspended at the moments when they were most needed. Just before the Civil War and then again afterwards, public debates on essential racial character paralleled discussions about the essence of money. Money took on the double-entendre association of metal and blood. Whenever precious metals ceased to serve as collateral for money's economic value and money's users were forced to trust in each other's rational motives, questions emerged about the nature of the species (people) using the money as well the nature of money itself (a specie). A species, after all, is a group of organisms categorized as similar enough to exchange genes and engage in breeding. Just as gold differed from other substances in the hierarchy of metals, it was believed, so too did the essential qualities of the races. The statesman John C. Calhoun, an infamous slavery advocate, went so far as to equate the blood of the nation to the money circulating in the body politic, as the historian Michael O'Malley observes:

> Think . . . of the extremely common metaphors comparing money, circulating through the nation, to blood circulating through the body. Thomas Hobbes understood money as the blood in Leviathan's body, and the metaphor served pro-slavery Southerner John C. Calhoun equally well nearly two hundred years later. "The currency of a country is to the community," Calhoun wrote in 1837, "what the blood is to the body . . . indispensable to all the functions of life." Pure blood, pure money: "Diluting the money supply diluted the nation's blood, and elevating the freeman depreciated the value of whiteness."[24]

The quality of blood (as of money) lay in its essential nature, which merely needed to be categorized and ranked. Mixing blood types could lead to pollution; purity had to be retained. Moreover, different types of bodies had varying capacities for autonomy, self-determination, and independence.

After the Civil War, the purity of money came into question. With the Legal Tender and National Currency Acts of 1862 and 1863, the government started printing "greenbacks" (paper currency without gold backing, also known as fiat currency). The debts of the war required the Treasury to produce more cash and consolidate control over the circulation of legal tender. Until that time, over five thousand types of state bank notes had been in circulation. Stores, businesses, churches, and other organizations had even issued their own paper currencies. But Viviana Zelizer explains, the postbellum state "taxed thousands of state-issued paper currencies out of existence."[25] As other sociologists such as Bruce Carruthers and Sarah Babb have noted, the state was also responding to public opinion regarding the impurities of this new currency, its dark power to deceive and shift shape and value arbitrarily.[26]

In *A History of Banking in All the Leading Nations*, William Graham Sumner recalled the opposition to a national banking system. It was partly a matter of the rights of each state being overwhelmed by the powers of the national sovereign, a sovereign that could not be trusted. According to Sumner: "One of [the] chief reasons for detesting the bank was that . . . it would help to support the conception of the federal Union as a confederated state with sovereign powers. Thus the bank was placed from the outset in the midst of the battle of State rights. [The bank would serve] an especially majestic and prerogative function of [the] sovereign."[27] President Abraham Lincoln, by contrast, regarded both the need for a national banking system and the move to the new currency as necessary evils, but also believed that, like many wrongs, this one could later be rectified. Reassuring Congress, Lincoln stated: "The suspension of specie payments [money backed by precious metals] by the banks [was] unavoidable. In no other way could the payment of the troops and the satisfaction of other just demands be so economically or so well provided for. . . . A return to specie payments, however, at the earliest period compatible with due regard to all interests concerned should ever be kept in view."[28] After Lincoln's assassination, the United States returned to a specie-backed currency and remained there until the monetary needs of the Vietnam War pressured the nation's coffers to give up on gold. War had transformed the state, and the state had provisioned war by making new types of money to finance it.[29]

Writing about the failure of Reconstruction, James Shepherd Pike used monetary metaphors to explain why racial inclusion polluted the body politic. He had initially sided with black suffrage and served as U.S. minister to the Netherlands during the Lincoln administration. When he returned to writing for the *New York Tribune*, he trained his attention on what he saw as the mess unleashed by the federal government's well-intentioned insistence that blacks and whites come together in democratic rule. Pike wrote that the Grant administration had ignored the *essential differences* between the races and allowed blacks to rule in South Carolina "by means of an alien and borrowed authority."[30] In *The Prostrate State: South Carolina under Negro Government,* Pike argued that elevating the ex-slave to full citizenship denigrated suffrage, deflating its worth to that of an *inflated bond.*[31] Having the federal government proclaim that black people were equal to whites in suffrage, in other words, was the same as having it declare "soft money" equivalent to hard coin. Both were aggressive political acts that polluted what had formerly been pure.

George Fitzhugh, a pro-slavery sociologist and author of *Sociology for the South* (1854) and *Cannibals All* (1857), had the "proof" that Pike needed. He argued that the belief that African Americans could work, save, and invest just as whites did rested on a dangerous fiction. Congress could not simply legislate a new nature upon the black species by bringing its members into a bank. As Fitzhugh observed with disdain, the "political economy stands perplexed and baffled in the presence of the negro. Capital can get no hold on him. . . . We must . . . expel nature before we can make negroes the equals of the whites."[32] In 1869, Maryland senator George Vickers insisted that "we cannot legislate into [Negroes] any fitness or qualifications which they do not now possess."[33] And observing how blacks interacted with money and banking seems to have offered proof in a natural setting of just how unfit they were for survival in an enlightened society.

CREATING COMMUNITY UNDER THE RADAR

Any claims that blacks lack a capacity for handling money and banking have to be made without reference to what they actually do with their money in the natural settings of work and home. According to Dylan Penningroth in *The Claims of Kinfolk,* enslaved blacks managed to accumulate assets and develop meaningful economic practices. A person who was marked as the property of a plantation owner still managed to lay claim to property. Such an individual marked the territory on which he lived as his own, engaged in community rituals that affirmed the boundaries of his property, and enjoyed the testimony of those who had seen the informal practices that indicated that the property belonged to him. It was such eyewitness accounts of ritual and exchange that blacks could provide to Union soldiers and their military courts as evidence of property losses or damages that required compensation.

By engaging in economic practices, blacks also changed their relationships with their oppressors. In one court hearing, for example, an Alabama county tax assessor testified on behalf of an ex-slave: "I know he had a horse. I never heard it disputed. If a negro in those days had a horse that was not his own, somebody would have disputed it sure."[34] In the 1860s and 1870s, blacks appealed to the Freedmen's Bureau, the Southern Claims Commission, and provost courts when seeking compensation for property confiscated during the Civil War. The claimants saw property as defined not by legal documents but rather by tradition and oral understanding. Moreover, they did not treat property as an individual possession in every case, but instead multiplied the rights of those who could lay a claim for ownership in the community.

Ex-slaves encountered trouble receiving compensation when they "valued some objects not only for their worth in exchange but also because those objects were enmeshed in a network of social relationships that made them personally and culturally precious."[35] A former slave by the name of Pompey Bacon, for example, wanted compensation for some white linens that he had set aside for his burial and thus considered culturally precious. This was a value claim that the courts would not recognize, however, as they regarded sentimental attachment as a weak basis for claiming a high price. Moreover, because they had belonged to a former slave, the material worth of the linens came into question. Goods were somehow less valuable by virtue of who had owned them and where they had been kept (outside a white household). In the end, the courts cared less about how the goods had been used than about how much could be gained from their exchange. All the same, the testimony supporting an ex-slave's claim sometimes carried the caveat that the property being claimed was of high quality "for a negro."[36]

Even historians and sociologists have discounted the value of black organizations and practices. In *An American Dilemma*, Gunnar Myrdal did acknowledge that black organizations had appeared in the civic landscape of U.S. society, but he portrayed them as failed attempts to mimic white organizations.[37] In his view, blacks were trying to imitate "forgotten relics" of white society that were no longer useful.[38] Late and lagging, they were authoring their own demise.

The historian Robert L. Harris rejects this view (and was not alone in doing so) and cites Ralph Ellison as support: "It is only partially true that Negroes turn away from white patterns because they are refused participation. . . . Men, as Dostoievsky observed, cannot live in revolt. Nor can they live in a state of 'reacting.'"[39] According to Ellison, blacks had created community institutions and benevolent societies that affirmed their sense of dignity and their insistence on living in liberty.

Indeed, between 1780 and 1830, blacks established credit unions, discussion groups, educational programs, and various benevolent societies and funeral groups to do practical things such as fund cemetery plots and funeral services, assist with medical expenses, help the disabled, offer comfort to those in distress, and provide insurance against food insecurity. As Harris points out: "Initiation fees and dues varied among [these associations], with a dollar to join and twenty-five cents a month dues as the norm. Payments for illness and burial likewise differed within the organizations. Some provided a flat payment of twenty dollars for funerals, while others agreed to provide the difference between costs and what the family could afford."[40]

These services should be partly understood within the context of the transition from slavery to freedom, during which the government did not offer blacks robust programs to help them enter the labor market or gather the small amounts of capital necessary for starting a business. Even before emancipation, the families of free blacks who had been kidnapped by bounty hunters from the South had needed financial assistance to find the victims and seek their release—hence the establishment in 1775 of the Society for the Relief of Free Negroes, Unlawfully Held in Bondage. Since members of this and similar societies sought the betterment of the race, they sometimes organized subcommittees on topics such as "*inspection* (to superintend morals, give advice, and protect from misfortune), *guardians* (to place children in apprenticeship positions to learn trades), *education* (to encourage instruction and to record marriages, births, and manumissions), and *employ* (to seek steady employment for free Blacks)."[41]

Some of these societies had moral prerequisites—that members be of good character, for example, or be "free from bodily affliction." Screening criteria helped determine who would be most likely to follow rules and least likely to make fraudulent claims that could drain the society's resources.[42] The 1823 constitution of the Brotherly Union Society in Baltimore, for example, included the clause: "No member shall be entitled to any benefit from the funds of this Society until he has been twelve months a member, and paid his dues for that time—if after that period affliction should render him unable to pursue his occupation or of gaining a livelihood for the space of eight days, he shall receive, during his affliction, two dollars per week—provided his sickness does not continue longer than three months."[43] While these rules shielded the societies from bankruptcy, informal monitoring practices during mandatory meetings and casual observations within the community also helped officers adjudicate claims by members.

Mexican Americans in the southwestern states likewise participated in burial societies and other benevolent groups, some of which operated under the aegis of the Catholic Church. One example of such were the lay brotherhoods, or confraternia, across the Catholic world. As we know from James Midgley, "in addition to their religious activities, they collected contributions from their members, which were used to assist the church's charitable work and to establish local orphanages, hospitals and almshouses."[44] Midgley's work on mutual aid societies and social policy reminds us that though some of these organizations were not official mutual aid societies, they could take on that function when the need arose. Indeed, such religious and community organizations, which operated beneath the radar of finance history, fulfilled banking services often denied or degraded for people of color or the working classes.

BANKING WHILE BLACK

As far as politicians were concerned, working, saving, and using a formal financial institution responsibly indicated a group's positive evolution toward full personhood and productive citizenship. Participation in a bank not only reflected but also shaped human character. With this in mind, the Freedmen's Savings and Trust Company was founded in 1865 to begin the process of financial inclusion for blacks. As it opened for business about a month before Lincoln's assassination, it was seen as the president's "last act of emancipation."[45] The Freedmen's Bank was in effect a philanthropic enterprise promoting character development and behavioral change. In the early twentieth century, the historian Walter Fleming explained its benefits:

> The negro put money in the bank during the summer and fall to be used in the winter and spring, when supplies were scarce. Thrift was encouraged; many negroes saved money to purchase homes, or to purchase farm stock and implements. The [bank] drafts, it is said, nearly always went for useful purposes. Less money was spent for liquors and for the worthless finery so dear to the African heart.[46]

According to Fleming, the emphasis lay on the utility of purchases and the shunning of frivolous items. Bank depositors who fit this mold were demonstrating their capacity to plan ahead and resist temptation in the here and now. The financial education provided by the bank thus constituted moral instruction and promised civic inclusion. If blacks could be incorporated economically into the United States in a way that demonstrated their equality with whites, their political rights would come to be seen as part of the natural order.

Between 1865 and 1874, Freedmen's Savings and Trust opened thirty-four branches in fifteen states as well as the District of Columbia. Robert Somers, a Scottish reporter who observed the branch in Charleston,

South Carolina, described its activities in *The Southern States since the War: 1870–1*, his study of the Reconstruction era:

> Go in any forenoon and the office is found full of Negroes depositing little sums of money, drawing little sums, or remitting to a distant part of the country where they have relatives to support or debts to discharge. . . . The Freedmen's Savings and Trust Companies do for the negroes what our National Savings Banks do for the working classes of England, Scotland and Ireland. . . . The negro begins to deposit usually with some specific object in view. He wishes to buy a mule or a cow, or a house, or a piece of land, or a shop, or simply to provide a fund against death, sickness or accident, and pursues his object frequently until it has been accomplished.[47]

Somers thus equated blacks with working-class whites in the United Kingdom, realizing that their financial activities and goals were identical when the institutional avenues to enact them were available. In the *Congressional Record* of 1874, Clinton Merriam, a U.S. congressman from New York, used the example of the Freedmen's Savings and Trust Company to demonstrate that African Americans could "engag[e] in 'self-making,' approaching equality by prospering and thereby forcing the nation to reconsider what racial difference meant."[48] In short, blacks were perfectly capable of demonstrating their thrift and readiness for the responsibilities of citizenship through their economic practices and the banking institutions that they patronized.

Frederick Douglass described the pride that he felt when seeing African American personnel and customers in an elegantly appointed bank. The magnificence of the building accorded with the majesty of a cathedral, and the respectable activities practiced therein reflected the moral and social ideals of economic incorporation into American society. As he recollected in *Life and Times, An Autobiography*:

> In passing [the bank] on the street I often peeped into its spacious windows, and looked down the row of its gentlemanly and elegantly dressed colored clerks, with their pens behind their ears and button-hole bouquets in their coat-fronts, and felt my very eyes enriched. It was a sight I had never expected to see. I was amazed with the facility with which they counted the money. They threw off the thousands with the dexterity, if not the accuracy, of old experienced clerks. The whole thing was beautiful. . . . When I came to Washington and saw its magnificent brown stone front, its towering height, its perfect appointments and the fine display it made in the transaction of its business, I felt like the Queen of Sheba when she saw the riches of Solomon, that "the half had not been told me."[49]

Like the Queen of Sheba, Douglass implied, one was likely to doubt the reports of the Negroes' advancement and their acumen in financial matters. Only after confirming these reports with one's own eyes would one realize that they actually understated the potential and moral standing of the Negro people, as evidenced by their bank.

By May 4, 1874, however, Douglass was struggling to rescue this symbol of thrift, moderation, and self-control. In a letter published in the *Baltimore Sun*, he noted that he had recently taken charge of the bank, that it had withstood three runs on its deposits in the last year and a half, and that he had just sent out a "quieting telegram" the night before, assuring the bank's depositors that in a few months the bank would be out of financial trouble, so long as the depositors exercised "a reasonable degree of patience." There was far more at stake than money, however, for the bank, as Douglass wrote, had been "especially established to encourage and assist the freedmen to save and increase their hard earned money, and thus to help them in the race to knowledge and higher civilization."[50]

The failure of Freedmen's Bank provided "evidence" that blacks were not ready for banking. Both W. E. B. Du Bois and Booker T. Washington recognized the symbolic violence caused by the bank's failure. Instead of talking about the bank as failing its black customers, newspapers and politicians seemed to blame blacks for trying to advance too far, and they warned blacks that any attempt to secure a better financial life would be impeded by those who make the rules. As Du Bois observed in *The Souls of Black Folk*, "Not even ten additional years of slavery could have done so much to throttle the thrift of the freedman as the mismanagement and bankruptcy of the series of savings banks chartered by the Nation for their special aid."[51]

Beyond the symbolic violence, the devastation on the ground was palpable. A deposition of one black bank depositor reveals just how dramatic the losses were for ordinary people.

About a week after the bank closed I carried my passbook up there, and also my little boy's. My little boy had $60 in the bank, I think, and I had nine hundred odd. I wanted to find out how I stood. I saw Boston [a swindler who worked at the bank] fifteen or sixteen times after the bank closed, and I waited and waited and waited, till at last I went to the bank to see about my book. I could not find Boston in, but I said to the clerk there, "Do you know how Watkins's account is?" He looked at the book and said, "Yes, you have 40 cents." I said, "Forty hells." He said, "Yes." Said I, "What will I do?" Said he, "I don't know . . ."

Question. I understood you to say that this money was the joint earnings of yourself and wife. *Answer.* Yes; she took in washing, and worked day and night, and I worked day and night, every day for the whole year. I have never been to a picnic or a ball since I have been in town.[52]

This couple worked without rest. They believed in the banking system and the promise of just reward for hard, dedicated effort. Extravagances were off limits; even a picnic seemed too lavish an expense. After doing everything by the book, they had discovered that the rules, not the rewards, applied.

Beyond these personal tragedies lay a collective debacle. For Douglass, when the bank crashed, "all the faith in saving went too, and much of the faith in men; and that was a loss that a Nation which to-day sneers at Negro shiftlessness has never yet made good." Similarly, Booker T. Washington saw the failure as leaving an imprint on blacks' understanding of what savings and banking should mean to them in America. "It was a long time after this," as Washington explained, "before it was possible to mention a savings bank for Negroes without some reference being made to the disaster of [the Freedmen's Bank]."[53]

For social Darwinists such as William Graham Sumner, racial hatred need not have had anything to do with the failure of the Freedmen's Bank since, in this view, institutions and groups of people undergo natural selection. Only the fittest survive. A student in one of Sumner's courses at Yale recalls how fiercely he believed in the free market's distribution of fair rewards to the striving and the best. Responding to a student's advocacy of government intervention in assistant industries, Sumner allegedly engaged in the following exchange:

"Professor, don't you believe in any government aid to industries?"

"No! It's root, hog, or die."

"Yes, but hasn't the hog got a right to root?"

"There are no rights. The world owes nobody a living."

"You believe then, Professor, in only one system, the contract-competitive system?"

"That's the only sound economic system. All others are fallacies."

"Well, suppose some professor of political economy came along and took your job away from you. Wouldn't you be sore?"

"Any other professor is welcome to try. If he gets my job, it is my fault. My business is to teach the subject so well that no one can take the job away from me."[54]

According to Sumner's logic, if one group of people find themselves with less capital than another, the disadvantaged group need not feel as

though the other has acted maliciously against them. Instead, each individual in each group has performed to the best of her abilities, and the
distribution of rewards reflects those natural talents. Sumner contrasted
the industrious versus the idle and the frugal versus the extravagant.[55]
When it came to questions of the fittest, the contrast lay less in the categorical exclusion of the fit from the unfit than in the notion that the
fittest come in a variety of dimensions and that some are far fitter than
others. (Such distinctions made about creditworthiness in the modern
economy will come up later.) Any attempt to change the competitive
market system so that the unfittest could thrive and the fittest would be
tamped down—"the socialist desideratum"—would follow the law of
anti-civilization.[56]

BANKING AND BELONGING

By removing from consideration the institutional rules, government
practices, and consequential narratives that privileged some players over
others, Sumner's notion of fitness made it harder to see the racialized
practices that shaped everyday banking experiences. The rules and prevailing beliefs allowed the enforcers of these practices to assume the moral
high ground while denying African Americans and other people of color
access to credit. Certain types of people simply did not deserve the benefit
of the doubt, as they had not shown themselves to be "fit" for independent
thought or the prudent management of money.[57] Following this logic, the
state should thus protect its population at large by not going too far in
recognizing the claims of the so-called unfit.

A new category of "fitness" for citizenship claims also emerged during
the Civil War. In exchange for going into battle, losing life or limb, citizens
found themselves with new social rights. The state provided pensions to
soldiers, life insurance to their survivors, and monetary compensation to
veterans who had lost their sight or mobility owing to war injuries. These
payments sent signals about who belonged to the nation and why.

This led to new opportunities for categorizing and scoring the credibility of citizens. The state had to differentiate the worthy from the
unworthy, the deserving from the undeserving. The pension application
screeners had to "guard against the 'cowards' and 'fraudulent malinger-
ers' who 'enlisted near the close of the war for large bounties and did
little actual service' [as] those who actually deserved pensions were 'the
real soldiers of the war' who had done 'patriotically what [their] duty
require[d].'"[58]

In this context too, blacks were not believed to be naturally inclined to
understand money or manage it well. One official who administered the

pension program noted that it was rare to find a black person who could be "counted reliable and absolutely truthful."[59] Blacks were also seen as easily duped. As the historians Larry Logue and Peter Blanck observe, these concerns (and other political motivations) doomed a campaign in the 1890s that would have provided a pension and bonus system for ex-slaves who had fought in the Civil War:

> The plan was never enacted, but Pension Bureau officials were sufficiently worried about confusion between existing and proposed pensions to order repeated investigations into the ex-slave plan's promoters. The promoters were "setting the negroes wild," wrote one investigator, "robbing them of their money and making anarchists of them." As an ex-slave pension association formed new chapters and pension advocacy spread by word of mouth, black veterans became emboldened to apply for Civil War pensions.[60]

It was believed that providing blacks with special monetary benefits would destabilize the entire government system. Liberty would be overtaken by license. Therefore, blacks could not be trusted; their applications needed extra scrutiny. Both their applications and their very persons suffered from what the African American studies scholar Eddie Glaude calls "the (racialized) value gap." They were evaluated by the color of their skin rather than the content of their capacities.[61]

Working-class immigrants also found themselves cast as bad calculators. As Zelizer notes in *The Social Meaning of Money*, charity organizations got involved in the money management practices of immigrants for fear that they were "unintelligent in the use of what they ha[d]" and easily tempted toward frivolous things that they could not afford:

> Consider the case of Mrs. C., a widow who had come from Italy to the United States. . . . When her husband died, their small savings were dissolved in doctors' bills and funeral expenses. In the early 1920s, the Columbus Family Service Society gave Mrs. C. and her six young children $10 a week in grocery orders to be spent at a designated grocery store. To prepare her for a money allowance, Mrs. C. was then asked to keep a written account of her purchases, watch grocery lists, and identify where staple foods could be bought cheaper. But when a visitor discovered that twenty-five cents recorded for tomatoes, supposedly canned, had been spent for one pound of fresh tomatoes— Mrs. C admitted she had been "extravagant" . . . the agency felt that she needed further training and supervision before being given a money allowance.[62]

To be considered competent and morally sound, an immigrant had to pay attention to the smallest of details. So long as she could prove herself to be disciplined, she deserved cash and the freedom to manage it. Not having this freedom, wrote Emma Winslow, a home economist of the period, would rob her of dignity and respect.[63] The immigrant's right to dignity, however, depended on her demonstration of merit.

Policymakers too played a role in promoting moral conduct among productive citizens. The Industrial Revolution had led to a structural shift such that "the average person had no assets whatever except his job. When that ceased, as it often did, he had no means. It was necessary for him to get credit until he could find another job." Predatory lending, in fact, was on the rise in this period, entrapping working people who had generally been thrifty and capable of resisting the temptations of extravagance. In 1911, Arthur Ham, director of the Department of Remedial Loans at the Russell Sage Foundation, traveled to a conference on charities and corrections in Augusta, Georgia, to propose that the fallout from predatory loans needed to be addressed. He saw predatory lending as "one of the greatest evils with which our cities have to contend" and called it a new "system of slavery." It was neither a matter of people seeking out loan sharks because they had a preference for high-cost, debilitating debt nor one of borrowers lacking self-control or moral fortitude. Ham explicitly stated that people who needed small loans were not lazy or spendthrifts. At the time, the annual earnings of workmen averaged $500; this amount, Ham argued, was not enough for an American family to maintain a modestly comfortable standard of living. Indeed, in an industrial society the average laborer was forced to borrow money whenever an illness or unforeseen crisis affected how much he earned or suddenly owed.[64] Despite having the evidence to make his case, Ham discovered that reason was not prevailing. Aside from the economic and political power wielded by various lenders, the moral meanings of debt and the characterizations of different types of debtors rooted in the minds of policymakers impeded the reform of short-term loans for the working classes, never mind people of color.

CREATIVE ADAPTATIONS, NOT MIMICRY

With good intentions, a number of public policy makers and financial educators tried to demonstrate that the poor and the working class lacked the kinds of financial institutions and resources available to the middle class. In their mind, if the same institutions and resources were available to all citizens, then goals and behavioral patterns would be identical across the population. Behaviors that did not conform to the imagined (white) middle-class template needed to be corrected so that families of color could enjoy the same opportunities as their white counterparts. Such correction would enable brown folks to leave the "backwardness" of their informal practices and institutions and mimic those of modernity.

One practice considered premodern (if not "backwards") was holding money. Instead of putting their money in a bank checking or savings account, some individuals paid a trusted community member to "hold money." The holder's job was to place the cash off limits, not simply to its owner but also to those who wanted to make claims on it, such as a spouse, a child, a parent or other relative, or a coworker. If asked, the money's owner could then credibly claim "not to have it."

But why pay an uninsured individual to hold money without the guarantees of a bank? Why miss out on an opportunity to build a banking and credit history? Was the practice merely a poor way of mimicking a savings institution? Or were there other social meanings and practices associated with holding money? Similar questions could be asked about funeral societies and other informal financial institutions.

If we compare debates on informal finance and formal banking with those on jazz and rule-bound (not improvised) music, we begin to see how easily creative adaptation was mistaken for badly executed imitation. In a 2014 article on John Coltrane in *The New Yorker*, Richard Brody explains that freedom in jazz means the right to cross-pollinate and dismisses the notion that John Coltrane's free jazz is merely "a lot of noise" — too free and unstructured to constitute "real" music:

> There's a temptation to consider free jazz as a freedom *from:* freedom from structures and formats and preexisting patterns of any sort. But it's also a freedom *to:* a freedom to musical disinhibition of tone, a vehemence and fervor, as well as a freedom to invent. The very word "freedom" meant something particular to black Americans in the nineteen-sixties. They didn't have it, and there's an implicit, and sometimes explicit, political idea in free jazz: a freedom from European styles, a freedom to seek African and other musical heritages, and, also, a freedom to cross-pollinate jazz with other arts. In the process, jazz musicians developed new forms and new moods that reflected a new generation's experiences and ideals.[65]

Similarly, informal finance reflects a yearning for freedom among many people, particularly those of color and immigrants without citizenship, who have their own understandings—however implicit—about finance as a social and political idea. Perhaps they too want the freedom to reject formal means of handling money that denigrate their own. Perhaps, as in music, they wish to cross-pollinate their financial traditions with those of formal institutions. Such blending could lead to a new movement, the development of novel forms, previously unrecognized sentiments, and meaningful opportunities that would reflect their understanding of what it means to live a good life.

CONCLUSION

The history of brown people's money has been clouded by the rhetoric of opportunity. After the Civil War, it was said, black and brown people could lift themselves up by learning how to save and be responsible consumers. After the First World War, blacks and Latinx could look to a sober life and the discipline required to build wealth on earth. After the passage of the Civil Rights Act of 1964, people of color as well as women found themselves not only equal under the law but, more importantly, equal in the eyes of banks and other financial institutions. Money was blind to race, religion, and creed and spoke only one language—that of mathematics. With all former barriers to participation in economic, political, and social life removed, any failure to save, invest, or live up to one's potential, it was argued, lay in the shortcomings of character, not color—that is, in individual actions, not institutional arrangements.

The rhetoric of opportunity proved powerful in cloaking the impediments to economic advancement. Money and property belonging to brown people were simply less attractive (and less secure) than the possessions of white people. As history advanced, racial tropes about the financial dealings of higher versus lower species came to be understood as color-blind views of responsible versus irresponsible consumers. Thrifty, self-controlled citizens seemingly accumulated savings through virtue, not politics. Given that opportunities lay waiting to be seized, poverty was a sign of a person's disregard for the higher life. Anyone with grit and determination who put forth adequate effort, so the reasoning went, would end up with sound finances. One of the core myths of the American Dream, as the political scientist Jennifer Hochschild put it, is that "virtue leads to success [and] success indicates virtue."[66] Yet financial institutions find it difficult to recognize some forms of virtue when practiced in communities of color.

Today a similar rhetoric of grit and hard work stifles progress toward credit justice. With blame placed solely on individuals and their character and drive, it becomes difficult to see alternative ways to apportion this blame (or what good such apportioning could do). The problem is compounded by the history of racial inequality that has constrained what individual drive can do, as well as by the rhetoric of individualism that hid those constraints. In *Divided by Color: Racial Politics and*

Democratic Ideals, Donald Kinder and Lynn Sanders define this dynamic as symbolic racism:

> A new form of prejudice has come to prominence, one that is preoccupied with matters of moral character, informed by the virtues associated with the traditions of individualism. At its center are the contentions that [people of color] do not try hard enough to overcome the difficulties they face and that they take what they have not earned. Today, we say, prejudice is expressed in the language of American individualism.[67]

Discussing this perspective in *Racism without Racists,* the sociologist Eduardo Bonilla-Silva concludes that as people articulate traditional liberalism ("work ethic, rewards by merit, equal opportunity, individualism, etc."), they also provide support for racially illiberal outcomes.[68] Traditional liberalism occludes the government's role in producing the very inequalities that individuals are asked to ameliorate.

This chapter has traced the chain of accumulating disadvantages that afflict families of color today. Along this chain we have seen the institutional rules and political maneuvers that have left people of color abandoned by the very government agencies charged with protecting them. But why should they protect from exploitation people who seem to seek exploitative services? Why should they treat such people as if they were capable of making sound decisions when the highest levels of government offer ample evidence of their lack of capacity in this respect? And why should they ask how existing community practices and beliefs could be mobilized for these people's benefit when they have already decided that such practices are backward or counterproductive?

Echoing C. Wright Mills in *The Sociological Imagination,* we argue that if in a country of 325 million only a few lack credit and the financial security it makes possible, we are merely dealing with a set of personal troubles. It is indeed only a matter of their moral character, their knowledge about finances, and the vagaries of chance that explain their financial insecurity. But when there are 45 million adults who lack credit, "that is an issue, and we may not hope to find its solution within the range of opportunities open to any one individual."[69] We need to keep history close at hand so that we can understand why the asset gap between people of color and whites has grown so wide, but we also need to understand how deeply the assumption of individual responsibility—the attitude that the solution to these public issues resides within individuals—underlies not only this history but the present-day experiences of individuals seeking credit.

There are some things that individuals cannot achieve alone. We need to recognize that disadvantaged people may also ascribe to traditional liberalism and take pride in their hard work and their sacrifices, even as they themselves recognize that their private troubles (low credit scores and money problems) have resulted from some rather public issues (banking practices, unfettered predatory loan providers, housing market discrimination, and the removal of enforced regulatory protections for first-time homeowners). They too want to live with dignity and be treated with respect, while demonstrating their commitment to honored ideals and their understanding of long-term constraints on advancement that they did not create as they work toward security and inclusion.

In the next two chapters, we delve into these public issues and the private lives they shape as we enter the lending circles at the Mission Asset Fund. We ask how new arrangements can transform who gets credit, how the newly integrated experience financial inclusion, and how they recognize the limits to inclusion because of other structural roadblocks.

Chapter 3 | Turning Disregarded Practices into Transformative Tools: Mission Asset Fund's Lending Circles

SOME FINANCIAL PRACTICES do not count toward a credit score because the person engaged in them happens to be on "the wrong side of the tracks." According to conventional wisdom, those on the right side are the people who open bank accounts and thus avoid check-cashing services and payday lenders; those on the wrong side use high-cost financial services or informal organizations that are not routinely tracked by credit scoring organizations. People who use these services miss important opportunities to avoid unnecessary fees and end up falling into debt traps.

Ending up on the wrong side of the tracks, however, is the result of social arrangements that diminish one side in favor of the other. Informal financial services are seen either as an impediment to full financial participation or as occupying a lower rung on the evolutionary ladder. Once an individual reaches high-level formal services, in this view, she should abandon the lowly services on which she has been depending. The old financial self must be sacrificed for the new self to be "born again." Nonetheless, the sacrifice can be humiliating, and the rebirth may require faith in the fanciful.

Is there another option? When developing the lending circles at Mission Asset Fund, José Quiñonez asked what would happen if those on the wrong side of the tracks became the cornerstone for a new kind of financial architecture. Why not count payments made into a funeral society or a rotating savings and credit association toward building a credit score? Informal practices such as these are by definition economic: they can be tracked and counted. If existing practices could be affirmed as such, the people who engaged in them would not have to sacrifice their sense of self. They would already be "saved."

During our interviews and observations at the MAF office, the clients we met told us that at MAF they learned that they did not have to become completely different people to pursue better financial lives. Before coming to MAF, they had grown accustomed to being told that everything they did was somehow wrong. They could not handle temptation; they did not save enough; they made themselves vulnerable to financial predators; and they lacked sound business sense. Weighed down by deficits, they failed to build assets. At MAF, however, they were being told that though history was not on their side, they could do something about it.

In this chapter, we give voice to MAF clients, the experts on their own lives and experiences.[1] We will learn about what it is like to face long-standing structural barriers to financial security while simultaneously being blamed individually for conditions that only government and well-resourced financial organizations could have prevented. Despite constraints beyond their control, many of the clients we met did recognize that they could change how they navigated such disadvantages, especially with help from MAF staff, who brought familiar practices into a new light and honored clients' decisions. It is this set of understandings that we will mine in this chapter.

COMMON EXPERIENCES
WITH FINANCIAL SERVICES

Doris, a client success manager at Mission Asset Fund, and Mohan, MAF's director of programs and engagement, visited the Young Families Resource Center on January 16, 2013. This San Francisco nonprofit serves teenage and young adult parents who have suddenly found themselves with new financial obligations, and Doris and Mohan were there to talk with them about the lending circles program.

Seven women were there for the session—not bad for ten o'clock on a weekday morning. At first, they sat in silence as Mohan spoke about some of the basic features of lending circles and the dates for new circles to be formed. Projected on the screen before them was an image of eight people seated in a semicircle, each stretching out their right hand to drop a dollar bill into a basket. The caption read: "Cestas Populares: Orientation & Formation." As Mohan explained, not only could the program help people get money when their turn came, but it could also improve their credit history.

One of the women in the room exclaimed, "Oh, it's a tanda!" Everyone began nodding in agreement. Responding to their simultaneous realization,

Doris interjected: "Let's say everyone puts in $100 and you have five people." The scenarios began to spin out. Among them was a doubter: "You're telling me I can have a credit score by doing the cesta thing?!" That sounded simply too good to be true.

Doris continued explaining the process: automatic deposits were made into the circle from members' bank accounts each month, with the lump sum delivered the same way. No time was wasted waiting for everyone to show up or chasing all circle participants to attend meetings together. MAF also guaranteed that if someone did not continue in the circle, the lump sum available would still be the same for those who remained.

The women then peppered Doris with questions: "Can it be less than $100?" "Can you participate in more than one?" "How do you get your number, your turn?"

Doris relied on the scenarios she had already heard from them to describe what they could expect from participating in the program. "Let's say that your car breaks down and you need it right away," Doris began. "Well, you can tell the group your situation and trade off with someone else in the group so that you can get the payment right away."

Now came the time for some impromptu storytelling. One woman said: "My boyfriend was in one of those, and he always wanted to get his share at the end. He'd say, 'What's the use of getting it up-front?'"

Doris confirmed his point: "So, you can use it as emergency or for savings. For example, people use it for vacations, graduation, presents during the Christmas season, or to pay off credit cards or personal loans."

But the enthusiasm sparked by these possibilities could not keep a common hurdle from emerging. As one woman confessed, "I don't have a bank account because I always get into trouble." This problem was not necessarily of her own creation. As another woman explained, "I *had* a bank account."

"Was it overdrawn?" the person beside her asked.

She looked up sharply, quickening her delivery. "No. It wasn't even overdrawn. I had over $100 in it. The bank said some info was missing or something. They sent me a check for the amount and closed the checking account out."

Doris acknowledged how difficult that experience must have been, and she offered a solution. "There is a community bank on Twenty-Ninth and Mission. They won't do you that way." Doris's expression implied that no one should be treated with such disregard.

Another woman in the room recalled prior problems with automatic payments that hit her account before the money had been deposited. There had been multiple fees for a single mistake, and it was not even clear that she was at fault as much as the bank teller claimed.

Doris noted that MAF's attitude was supportive rather than disciplinary. "If you have a financial hardship, call us. There will be a $10 fee, but we get charged $35 from Citibank. We only charge the $10 so people will take responsibility, but we don't charge you the entire amount of the fee that we face if you don't have the money in your account. We'll take you aside and work with you to get current." Doris presented a model of banking in which the lender shares the fines of the borrower—a true example of shared responsibility. The group seemed to agree that fees were expected, but how much was sufficient? The fees came from the very source that consumers were supposed to trust. It's one thing to be overcharged by a payday lender or a loan shark; it is quite another thing when the charges come from Wells Fargo.

Greg, one of the men we interviewed later, recounted his experience with his checking account at Wells Fargo. "We had to check [the account] often because sometimes they'd take out some money that we didn't know about." Greg believed that some of the overdrafts on his account stemmed from Wells Fargo imposing fees on the account that caused his balance to be inadequate. To men like Greg, mainstream financial actors seemed to act with impunity. It was hard to gather evidence to prove wrongdoing, and even if the evidence seemed clear, who would care? Perhaps, he reasoned, a nonprofit would be better.

"YOU DECIDE"

Four days after witnessing Doris and Mohan in action, we attended an information session at Operation Hope in Oakland. Joel Lacayo, manager of the MAF lending circles program at the time, led a conversation that was less about concerns over exploitation and more about an insistence on respect. On the screen in a packed room was a photo of Joel's three-year-old son, dressed in dark denim overalls with soft white pinstripes and a white undershirt with a yellow-and-blue bowtie printed on its collar. Clearly Joel was a proud father who knew that he was facing a room filled with other proud parents and grandparents, as well as a few single people looking for a way to do and be better.

"What can you do with $100 a month as an individual?" Joel asked. "Seriously? Okay, you can save it and see how it accumulates over a few months, but we all know how after two or three months something happens along the course of you saving, right? So you have to start all over again because it's difficult to build savings. But let's say, instead, if we all have $100 and we pool the money."[2] The theme of life's unpredictability and tendency to waylay even the best-laid plans popped up again and again. So too did the message that *there is another way.*

Joel continued: "So a lot of you or some of you probably haven't had bad experiences with this type of lending outside of us? Or maybe you have heard of family or friends doing this kind of lending but having people not pay some months or the last person not getting the full lump sum, if anything, right?"

Someone in the audience called out, "Yeah, I've done this with my own family."

"And what happened?" Joel asked.

"Well, life."

"Exactly!" Joel said with his arm outstretched and a knowing nod, confirming that their fear that others might not follow through was real. "All of a sudden, somebody couldn't commit. Something happened, and they had taxes or something, and they just couldn't commit and so they just couldn't."

"So what ends up happening with the pot of money you're supposed to get?" Joel continued. "Well, essentially they're unable to do it, or they keep on saying that they will, but they don't follow through."

Joel reassured them that they could avoid this common problem by participating in an MAF lending circle:

> Our organization actually guarantees all the money in the pot. If everyone else except me, for example, cannot continue paying into the circle for legitimate reasons, our organization will be willing to work with them to work something out and then make arrangements one-on-one with them. I've told you that out of the five and a half years that we've been doing this, only six people have not been able to pay us all back the entire amount, or we had maybe around fifteen people that have to do payment arrangements on the side, and they've paid us successfully after that. Let me also tell you that when a person has to drop out, we don't report negative information to the credit bureaus. We only report them positively for the months that they paid. Once they cannot continue, we remove them based on their request and the financial situation that they're going through and discontinue reporting them, but we do not continue reporting them incorrectly or negatively or in default because we have already removed them from the loan itself.

Turning to questions about the program's month-to-month operations, he began using the refrain "You decide."

"How much would the monthly payment be?"

"You decide."

"How many people in a circle?"

"You decide."

"What's the maximum monthly payment?"

"You decide."

"Can the order in which lump sums are received be changed?" (Approximately 40 percent of the clients we interviewed either witnessed or participated in a swap of payout order.)

"You decide."

The phrase "you decide" allowed the participants to reply in unison with Joel as he answered questions with a conspiratorial nod. They knew the answer even before hearing the question: they could decide how to manage their own financial lives.

They were ready to join.

THREE PROGRAMS

According to the Mission Asset Fund website, lending circles not only place clients in the driver's seat but also allow the very programs to which these clients gain access to "build on the strengths of [their] communities." MAF, in fact, runs three lending programs using the Salesforce cloud platform:

Lending circles: "Across the world, friends and family come together to lend money to each other. . . . With Lending Circles, we've transformed this practice into a safe way to build your credit." There is no interest on the loans distributed through lending circles, and these social, credit-building loans can be taken out in amounts up to $2,400, for any purpose.

Business programs: "Whether you're developing a business plan, starting to build your business, or you've been in business for years, Lending Circles for Business offers loans to help you finance any business expense while building your credit." MAF business loans for starting or expanding a business, in amounts up to $2,500, are also interest-free.

Immigration programs: "Applying for immigration relief can be expensive. Our program offers an affordable way to fund your USCIS application fee while building your credit." MAF offers these interest-free loans to cover the U.S. Citizenship and Immigration Services (USCIS) filing fee that must be paid by immigrants applying for citizenship ($725), for adjustment of their status for a green card ($1,225), or for renewal of their Temporary Protected Status (TPS) ($495).[3]

Lending circles vary in size, but usually include six to twelve people. The loans, or payouts, can be as low as $300, but most of the circles have ten participants contributing $100 per month, with $1,000 payouts.

Potential clients fill out an application (see appendix B) and take an online financial education course to qualify for participation. Once they form a circle, they look at the loan documents, noting the number of payments required, the deadlines for making them, and the consequences of late payment.

To participate in the program, applicants must have access to the internet, an active email account, a checking account, and either a Social Security or an individual tax identification number. The obligatory government-issued identification can be a driver's license, passport, state or city ID card, or identification issued by a consulate. Proof of income may be a pay stub showing two consecutive months of earnings or a bank statement recording a three-month record of deposits. A letter certifying that a person receives benefits, including the exact amount of the benefits, also suffices. The flexibility of these requirements allows immigrants, the self-employed, and others with nontraditional incomes to participate in MAF programs.

Using the cloud platform Salesforce to process its social loans has enabled MAF to develop a national network of more than fifty lending circle providers across seventeen states and Washington, D.C. Moreover, MAF was given ten free licenses in 2007 as part of Salesforce's commitment to donate 1 percent of its product, 1 percent of its equity, and 1 percent of its time to philanthropy.

LEARNING WITHOUT EMBARRASSMENT

We were particularly interested in the financial education available to program participants, both informally and formally. MAF offers in-person as well as online courses on topics ranging from budgeting and credit management to debt and banking. Although we neither measured the financial knowledge of participants nor evaluated the effectiveness of MAF courses, we did discuss with participants how their new financial knowledge fit with what they had already been doing in their everyday financial practices prior to joining their lending circle.

MAF clients certainly did not emerge from some kind of financial wilderness in need of being "civilized" through education. Instead, they told us, they experienced the lending circle as an opportunity to refocus attention on their finances and build on practices that they had developed over their lifetime. As Angela explained, "I think recently I did the checking [class], how to use my checking, or was it my credit card? Something like that. I think it's something that I already learned, I already knew in the past, and I'm already practicing, but it just kind of reminds me again, that if you just keep doing that, then—[it] kind of revalidates what I've already been doing."

Margarita came to the financial management class at the Mission Asset Fund not expecting to be asked to speak. This was, after all, a preliminary training session for all those who wished to join circles. The experts stood at the front of the room while the learners, prepared to listen to them, took their seats. "That's not how we do things here," Joel Lacayo told them. "You have things to teach yourselves and each other." The experts were there not to impose a completely different set of practices on them or berate them for bad financial behavior in the past, but to get them to think about the positive things they could do.

Joel used his own financial story as a relevant example to which the clients could relate: "If you carry a little balance [on your credit card], it's not that big of a deal in terms of how much you pay in interest, so don't beat yourself up. Just understand what the ideal is and work on getting there in time." He admitted that navigating the formal financial system did not come naturally to him, even though he had once worked for a bank and his father was an accountant who worked on budgets for a living. "I never asked him about these things," Joel told the group. "I was just paying minimum [on my credit cards] and got myself into [thousands of dollars of] debt."[4]

Consumer finance research has often underscored the importance of financial education and literacy for consumers trying to reach their financial goals. Indeed, much ink has been spilled on what people *don't know* about their money or the operations of the financial system.[5] All too frequently, these discussions fall back on the question of "personal responsibility" and focus on poor decisions made by the economically struggling. Our interviews, however, did not bear this out. On the contrary, our interviewees revealed knowledge and demonstrated financial skill sets that, while not perfect, did give them a basis on which to build.

In many respects, the participants we met—even those who were "underbanked" or credit-invisible—resembled consumers up and down the income scale. Although some admitted gaps in their knowledge, the financial classes were not educating them from scratch but rather expanding on things that they already knew and helping them refine practices in which they were already engaged. The classes thus served as an opportunity for MAF members to redouble their efforts, often after a discouraging setback.

Based on our analyses of the interview data, Tina's experience is representative of the experiences of many whom we met. She had already done her best to pay off her credit card debt in a timely fashion, and now the financial management class, she told us, had pushed her to set new goals:

> With my habit, I always want to pay on time, but now I can look for—let's say I was going to apply for another credit card—I can look for the one that is able to stretch for fifteen months or twelve months without APR. And I want to pay not the minimum, but at least 50 percent of whatever I need to buy, in a large amount, and not to have it late. So it was like understanding these fine prints and everything like that.

When asked later in the interview what she had learned from her lending circle experience, she specifically stressed the importance of the financial management class: "I know that I do have good spending habits. I'm actually very frugal, maybe not cheap, but frugal. . . . I would [say]. After the classes about credit, savings, and all that, I'm more *aware* [emphasis added] of it. But maybe my spending habit wouldn't change— it's just being more aware of the finances." Similarly, Yasmeen, when asked about her general experience with the course, replied: "I believe a lot of this, a lot of it, I kind of had a concept of it before. It's just kind of more into my head of eliminating, again, expenses, and basically like, paying [on time], instead of paying all these fees, like the credit card fees and all that stuff."

THE USUAL PRACTICES

For some clients, lending circles resonate with past practices; for others, they reflect the behavior of "everyday" people like themselves. Among our interviewees, over 70 percent had some prior experience with a lending circle, in that they or someone they knew had already partici- pated in one. Only a small fraction of those familiar with the practice had concerns about losing money. One of them, Maria, expressed genu- ine reservations about the people who participated in them. She saw them as desperate and therefore forced to do it and spoke with anxiety about the possibility that "people might run off with your money." MAF, however, had allayed her fears. "Well, it's nothing like that here," she assured us.

The practices were not merely familiar to participants but resonated with community life and culture for them. Even though Tina, like Maria, was initially suspicious, she knew that her mother had participated in a variant on the lending circles in her village in Honduras, as had her part- ner. "It's all on paper," she said about the circle in which her partner par- ticipated. "Like, there's no funny thing in the background, or people doing stuff, or taking money out of your bank without you knowing it. So I'm like, okay, maybe I'll give it a try."

MAF clients did not anticipate a sharp learning curve during a lending circle startup and felt confident that they could do it without much trouble. As Dora told Marlene, who conducted our interviews, financial practices do not have to be taught formally but can be picked up from day-to-day experiences:

DORA: When I was younger, I remember my parents did tandas . . . it's like lending circles . . . pretty much the same thing— just not formally reported to credit bureaus and stuff like that.

MARLENE: What are some of the things that [your parents] would tell you about it?

DORA: They wouldn't. I would just see it. I would just see it. They would take me . . . my mom never really had a day care or anything like that to take me . . . and I would see them exchanging, and I kind of knew what was going on. And then, eventually, I heard words like tanda, and they would choose . . . who would get it first, second, third, fourth, fifth, and all that stuff.

Keisha had similar memories:

I sort of understand the concept of the program because I'm from the Caribbean, and my father and his siblings have participated in something called Susu. . . . So you could take the first hand or you could take the last hand, but you keep paying until it goes around for everyone and then you can keep doing it and doing it and doing it. And a lot of people from the island of Trinidad, when they come here, that's how they acquire homes and save money and things like that.

Even if lending circle participants had had trouble dealing with banks and credit scores, they were certainly good with money when engaging in tandas and susu.

According to the French sociologist Pierre Bourdieu, when people think that they are bad with money, the belief "goes without saying" and remains unchallenged because "it comes without saying."[6] Being good with money seems to them to be a natural talent rather than a learned practice, and the ways in which monetary practices are organized likewise appear to follow a natural hierarchy from informal to formal. But such "natural" arrangements do not acknowledge and institutionalize the day-to-day practices of people with limited means.

Part of the problem lies in the view that turning to a rotating savings and credit association is a practice of last resort. Some members of the MAF lending circles spoke about past experiences with ROSCAs at times when they had been unbanked and unbankable. "When my mom brought me and my older brother to the U.S., I was three years old," Fernando told us. "We were unbankable for the first six years, I think, of our time in the U.S. My family did a lot of progressing through a lot of [informal] lending circles. . . . That's what my mom used to do back when she was in the textile industry in New York." Despite acknowledging a lack of other options, individuals also expressed pride in their self-reliance and their ability to make a way—as the saying goes—out of no way.

Learning the Game

A central theme emerging from our interviews was that MAF participants, despite their occasionally tenuous connections with mainstream financial services, faced many of the same struggles and hurdles as other Americans, though often with less room for mistakes. In fact, these respondents experienced so much less room for mistakes that some of them preferred to disregard their finances and look ahead to the future without much reflection.

Maria, for example, told her interviewer that her financial goals had changed during her time in the lending circles, and that a friend had suggested to her that she seek help from Suze Orman, the financial adviser and motivational speaker. But Maria was not interested: "I knew who she was, but it freaked me out because I didn't want to hear about finances. I didn't want to talk about it. I didn't want to hear anybody. I kind of hated Suze Orman, not even knowing, just because she talks about finances." Maria admitted, however, that her student loans had ballooned and that she had sunk into a depression and really did not want to think about her finances. This is an altogether common experience among consumers everywhere, not just those who are struggling.

Studying responses by Scandinavian and American investors to different types of information, the social scientists Niklas Karlsson, George Loewenstein, and Duane Seppi identified a tendency to avoid distressing or potentially distressing information.[7] Calling this the "ostrich effect," they noted that people are "likely to delay acquiring information, even when [it increases] the quality of decision making." If such information requires them to confront and internalize disappointments that they prefer to avoid, they will do their best to ignore it.[8] The desire to ignore past financial problems expressed by some of the MAF clients is comparable to the ostrich effect, which is common among people across the income and educational spectrums.

Pairing the financial management classes with the delivery of social loans may have made it easier for clients to focus on modifying some of their financial habits. Mauricio, for instance, remarked that his financial behavior changed after the class. "I changed it, it changed. You had to be more cautious with the expenses, to set up budgets and all, right? Because sometimes when you don't have [enough money], you're not paying attention to [your budget] and you have the credit card and so you spend. We have never been [in] arrears, we paid everything every end of the month, or when it was due. Right now, we're paying everything because I think we are controlling [our spending] a little more."[9]

When in-person financial management classes were held in 2013, we were able to observe what people asked and how much they were told more generally about the financial system. Two important questions that arose were whether clients should carry a balance on their credit cards (no), and how a credit score was calculated. During the training, clients were presented with a pie chart that broke down their FICO score:

History of payment: 35 percent

Amount of debt: 30 percent

How long the participant had had credit: 15 percent

How much new credit the participant had: 10 percent

Types of credit: 10 percent[10]

They learned that they could improve their credit score simply by reducing the amount of debt they carried relative to available credit. A knowledge of such percentages and the "rules of the game," however, could only come from an expert. MAF clients were therefore told not to be surprised that they did not automatically know the ins and outs of strategically taking on and paying back debt.

Closing Accounts

On September 16, 2013, a client called the MAF office a little after 10:00 AM to speak to Mohan about a missed payment. She hoped that, owing to her relationship with Mohan, the missed payment would be forgiven and she could avoid all fees. In responding, Mohan took care to demonstrate that the client still had some control over how the situation would be resolved, but that the rules about imposing fees had to be applied fairly across all clients:

> If we were to delay the payment for your account, we'd have to do it for everyone else. If you're not able, we'll re-debit your account at the end of the month. It will be your regular monthly payment plus the $10 late fee. That's separate from any insufficient fund fees that your bank might charge. If you can go ahead and deposit money into your account, that's a way to make sure you can avoid that. But it sounds like you have another question as well.[11]

In asking about the client's other concerns, Mohan recognized that she was a person with a full life that she was managing as well as she could. Directing the conversation with the client, he explained the fee that MAF imposed as well as the fee charged by her bank. Mohan emphasized that her well-being was more important than the fact of the missed payment. The phone call thus offered the client an opportunity to plan for the future in a less than ideal situation but with support.

Even with such support, some clients found the requirements of the lending circle daunting. For example, Mohan recalled trying to help Benji get back on track to make on-time payments, but the young man eventually had to drop out of the program. He had tried to apply to MAF's Dreamers program, which uses the lending circle payout for fees for college-age youth applying to Deferred Action for Childhood Arrivals (DACA) through the federal government. Because Benji's family had a history of domestic violence and had also suffered trauma while fleeing their country of origin, he did not have the support needed to gather the documentation required or overcome the strain of managing multiple obligations.

> When Benji missed a payment, [we had] conversations about how to get back on track, and "How can we support you?" And then [we discussed whether to make] that ultimate decision to withdraw, and what was the best choice for him. So I, of course, wanted him to continue. I have a certain investment in seeing participants continue, but [my role was] helping him walk through what's the best for him at this time and recognizing and understanding that [leaving the program] was the best choice for him and supporting him in that and talking [it] through. "Okay. How will this appear on your credit reports? And what's the benefit of the payments that you made on time, and how have you developed this positive credit history? The credit history won't be as significant as it would have been had it continued throughout the course of the loan because there won't be as many payments that you have made. But it'll appear as an account closed, and the loan's been paid off."

Mohan regarded Benji's withdrawal from the program as a learning opportunity—something that would help him when he went on to apply for other loan products in the future. He hoped that Benji had received the support he needed to "quit" without being made to feel like a "quitter." As Mohan explained: "His withdrawal, to me, doesn't mean that he failed, or he didn't succeed, or that our program wasn't a success. One of the goals of our program is to provide a means for folks to be able to learn these financial skills, and he was able to do that. He didn't complete the loan, but maybe he didn't need to." Rather than hound Benji to finish the program, Mohan affirmed that, with a little support, he could get back in control. As seen in the photographs section in the back of this book, Mohan, José, Doris, and other staff members appear in ongoing relations with the members of MAF as they gained greater visibility and experienced the highs and the lows.

Would more loans be paid back if people were treated with greater respect? Would it be possible to come to a consensus that a recognition of people's circumstances and a willingness to work with them toward a mutually agreeable outcome would increase support for and trust in formal financial service providers?

COORDINATION COSTS

As noted earlier, unlike many interventions that require multiple meetings at an agency or appointments with staff, MAF makes a point of reducing clients' transaction costs by limiting the number of times they need to travel to an office or take time off from work and family. A new lending circle participant meets only once with other participants, usually in the Mission Asset Fund office, to form a lending circle. Those who are not taking online financial management classes can also meet prior to the lending circle formation session to participate in a workshop. Because payments and lump sums are delivered electronically, participants do not meet in person each month. Many of them appreciate not having to schedule one more thing each month, as their jobs often require them to come to work on short notice. When budgets are tight and time is in short supply, coordinating who stays home with the kids and the best way of traveling from one job to the next can leave little time to attend an unnecessary meeting.

Ironically, the very thing that helps MAF clients participate in the program can also bring dissatisfaction. Some clients actually wish it were more social—a place offering ongoing support. As Michelle told us:

I haven't been in touch with the other members of the group. My first visit was to learn about how this works, and the second visit was to receive the classes. I liked the classes; that day I spoke with people who were not in my group. I had a very nice evening with the people here; they are from many countries. The second time I participated in group savings here at lending circles, it was the same experience. Some people are now acquaintances and we share a quick "hi." The next time I came in, I was not able to talk to anyone since I was busy with work.

Yet, though Michelle said she wanted more contact, she admitted that sometimes her busy schedule precluded it.

Cynthia was working through a midlife personal debt crisis and finding it tough to coordinate her responsibilities: "I have so many things to pay out that [the timing] threw me off. . . . It set me back. I had to pull out financially from the . . . debt relief program." Jim, another client, recalled wanting to pay a parking ticket as soon as it arrived in the mail, but his wife reminded him that bills arrived in the mail all the time: "Something will come in the mail, and we'll be screwed over budget-wise. I'll just wait till the end of the month and then I'll pay it. Can't get any surprises." One client indicated that she did not want to carry credit cards because she couldn't keep up with them: "I have too much going on right now, and I know it's going to come to a point where I am going to have one, but I don't need a lot of stuff going on at once. I really don't. I tried that. I did it, but it wore me out because I have to keep track of my money as well." In short, every bill and every meeting represents yet one more thing to coordinate, and potentially one more obligation to miss.

CONCLUSION

The lending circles represent an assertion of citizenship from below. By this we mean that these clients organized their own lives and made independent decisions about how to care for themselves and their loved ones while belonging (through their credit scores) to a community of both ranked and unrankable consumers. It mattered to them to see that their community's practices and values were reflected in the financial marketplace. And although they were not equal in their credit scores, they were equal in their insistence that they be judged by the content of their actions rather than by the side of the track (formal or informal) where they performed those actions.

The challenge lay in the benefits of citizenship. Clients with a high credit score found themselves grappling with what new offers for participation would mean and how much they would cost. By becoming visible, they also became targets for indebtedness. Hence, we turn to the meaningful tension that results from being counted.

Chapter 4 | Becoming Creditable, Being an Equal

"WHAT'S YOUR NUMBER?" In the United States, creditworthiness is repre-
sented by a concrete score. Depending on the algorithm used by a particular credit reporting agency, individuals generally find themselves
associated with several different numbers, ranging from 300 to 850. They
may also have no score, meaning that for them there is no record of their
engagement in any of the various activities, such as getting a car loan or
making credit card purchases, that show up on a credit report. Most of the
participants in lending circles to whom we spoke were keenly aware of
whether their score fell within the prime, subprime, or no-score range even
if they did not know the precise figure.

The notion of creditworthiness also has less tangible aspects; certain
social meanings are attached to credit, which our respondents discussed
with us. For some, the number conveys where they stand in relation to other
markers of independence and adulthood. For others, it signals responsibility and a sense of purpose. A good credit score can also represent inte-
gration into a new country and culture—a shift from being "invisible"
to "visible."

For all of us, increasing our credit score requires that we engage in activities that are part and parcel of a particular form of capitalism that we may
find complex, opaque, or even distasteful. It may mean reengaging with
institutions that once treated us with disrespect or outright dishonesty.
It may mean attaching hopes and dreams to a promise that a high credit
score alone cannot deliver. And it may mean being taken advantage of not
only by banks and other lenders but also by those closest to us, friends and
family, who ask, "Can you co-sign a loan agreement?" "Can I borrow your
credit card?" "Can you take this loan out on my behalf?" Of course, what
good is financial security if we cannot help those we care about? Yet how
much help can we extend before spiraling into the very trouble that an

improved credit score has helped us escape? In short, the social meanings of credit are complex and fraught with tension.

In this chapter, we look at how lending circle participants speak about credit, both generally and with regard to their own specific scores and experiences with credit.[1] The language that people use to speak about their credit reflects their desire to gain access not only to the mainstream financial system but also to many other meaningful aspects of American life, such as ownership of homes, businesses, and cars. Good credit equals opportunity and signals passage into adulthood. But ambivalence toward the credit system in the United States is also rampant. Past experiences with the financial system may have been less than good, and other structural and personal challenges beyond increasing a credit score can keep people from attaining these goals.

As noted, creditworthiness allows individuals to move toward visibility. At the same time, financial systems and markets are not structured to grant full financial citizenship to everyone. Indeed, the "right to belong"— one of the components of financial citizenship—is complicated. Although we consider the ability to spend money on friends, family, and community dignity-affirming, we also note that there are ways in which family and significant others can get in the way of achieving goals and reaching "creditability." The "you decide" mantra used by MAF staff in lending circles is laudable, but durable disadvantages that have accumulated for a long time remain, and no single individual as force of will can vanquish them.

BECOMING RESPONSIBLE AND BECOMING VISIBLE

When José Quiñonez and other MAF staff talk about their program's mission, they often invoke the metaphor of making the invisible visible. Some participants had picked up on this phrase; speaking to us about their experiences with lending circles, they pointed to themselves as those who were "invisible" to creditors. As one woman put it, she and her husband were "not on the radar" of the American financial system. Although they had no debt, they had not used any financial products or engaged in the kinds of transactions that contribute to building a credit score. So when she wanted to buy a car, the dealership pulled her credit report and denied her a loan, citing her poor score. Rather than placing her "not on the radar," her low score had flagged her as someone to watch out for, someone who could not be trusted to make a repayment or perhaps even should be penalized with a high-interest loan and additional penalties. A higher score would have erased this kind of stigmatized invisibility, opening up access for her to the products offered to "responsible" individuals. An example like hers offers a slightly different way of looking at the visible/invisible dichotomy.

Good credit often signals more than a person's sense of responsibility. Like graduating from high school or college, getting married, or holding a steady job, having good credit is viewed by some as yet another marker of reaching adulthood. David, for example, had a job that allowed him to meet his "basic needs," but at some point in the near future, he observed, "I'm going to have to get a car loan and a mortgage. Be an adult." For him, a good credit score was crucial for achieving these goals; without one, he risked being denied loans and mortgages or charged higher fees.

The financial system, however, sets many obstacles on people's path to what they view as responsible adulthood. Preying on their inexperience, the system may set them up for failure at the very moment when they are transitioning into adulthood. The complexity of the system may even seem rigged against them. Finally, the credit system may fail to recognize their contributions and erase their accomplishments because these do not fit into certain boxes. Participation in programs like the MAF lending circles helps repair some of the damage done by the financial system, but confidence in one's financial management skills and a higher credit score by themselves may not buffer everyone from future negative experiences.

Burned as a Young Adult

How do MAF participants go about establishing or repairing credit? In addition to receiving and paying back their social loan, those who do not have a credit card may be advised by MAF staff to apply for one. Obtaining a credit card, making purchases, and paying balances in a timely fashion can be an easy way to start boosting a credit score. Like others with poor credit scores, MAF participants may be able to obtain a secured credit card, one that requires a deposit to the creditor in return for securing a line of credit. (The credit card company can use this deposit to pay for missed payments.)

Credit card companies have nevertheless been a source of financial problems for more than a few MAF participants, such as Michelle. She described herself to us as a first-generation college student for whom "making the transition from going to school and then entering into the work field was really difficult." She was employed at one time, but a series of low-paying, unstable jobs did not enable her to earn enough money to afford the cost of housing in the area. After shuttling from one sublet to another, Michelle found herself homeless. Some of her financial difficulties began while she was still in college. As she noted, credit card companies "sit on your college campus. . . . That's how they got me." Michelle also claimed that the issuer of her first credit card did not correctly explain the company's terms and conditions.

When the school year begins, college campuses are, in fact, littered with small tents where newly arriving students can sign up for credit cards. The Credit Card Responsibility and Disclosure (CARD) Act placed tighter regulations on how these companies conduct business with students. (For example, they can no longer offer gifts such as T-shirts or mugs as enticements for signing on.) Yet despite these regulations, more than forty-five thousand new college accounts were opened in 2012.[2] On their own for perhaps the first time, and with little knowledge of how to manage a credit card, college students are ripe for accruing significant debt relative to their income and maxing out their credit cards. As a consequence, many will graduate not only with student loans to pay off but also credit card debt.[3]

After paying down her balances, but prior to enrolling in MAF, Michelle canceled all her credit cards. She referred to herself as an impulsive spender who bought items that she did not need or could not afford. Credit cards enabled this behavior, and with the high interest rates on her balances, she ended up owing more in interest than on the actual charges. After acquiring the financial education offered by MAF, however, Michelle came to believe that she could keep her spending under control and use a credit card to help her achieve her goals. Nonetheless, her past interactions with the credit system had left her scarred.

Michelle's experience was not unique. Keisha recounted what happened to her during her first year at college:

> At certain times of the year, they'd have all these credit card people out there, and they'd give you credit very easily, even though you were a student. You got the Visa card, the Discover card, very easy, for just a bag of M&Ms. You had no job per se, you're at college. You had no job. So you started off bad. You couldn't afford to have those credit cards in the first place. So when you have credit people on the grounds of college campuses, they're doing a disservice to the students that are there, a disservice, because some of us, we already come out of school with debt from our student loans and then it's compounded. We feel we can buy things now or spring break—we're going on vacation and we don't have money . . . well, I didn't. I only speak for myself; I didn't have money to maintain those credit cards at all.

Young people are targeted by credit card companies in other ways besides visits to college campuses. As these companies develop more sophisticated algorithms, they are able to tailor their products to more and more people who would previously have been deemed a credit risk. Twenty-five years ago, a young high school graduate with a low-paying job would have probably never received any credit card offers. Today, however, a creditor can access a great deal of personal information on various segments of the credit market and design a credit card with a low limit (for example, $500) but an extremely high interest rate and various fees and penalties for late payment and other infractions. Companies have figured out how to offer products that allow them to make profits while placing much of the risk on cardholders. One participant, Maria, described being deluged with credit card offers as a young adult:

> At some point, I had about eight or nine [cards]. Because, I mean, I was so young, and they started sending me credit cards from everywhere: Nordstrom's, Macy's, Mervyn's. I had every credit card, and I just felt like I was so young, and I lived on my own, and I wanted to look good and buy things that young people want to buy, and then I just, I felt like, "Wow! Everybody wants to give me credit," and I didn't even know what that was. Or—I don't know, I was just very young and naive and so . . .

Youth and naïveté are not mere excuses. Brain-imaging studies show that the brain is not fully formed until one's midtwenties. In fact, the prefrontal cortex, the region that plays a key role in decision-making, impulse control, and logical thinking, is one of the last areas to develop.[4] It may therefore be unrealistic to expect young adults to be ready to make "responsible" financial decisions without guidance. Our culture, however, tends to blame individuals for failures related to money and credit management, regardless of their age. Yet placing the blame on the "naive," the "impulsive," or those who go on vacation without the money to pay for it ignores the role of the financial system in creating such pitfalls. As Jim, another MAF participant, admitted, young people like him should not be able to "get a credit card until [they're] ready, until [they're] more financially stable, ready to be an adult. The first time I got my credit card I was swipe, swipe; I didn't think about the repercussions."

Moreover, the maturity and knowledge that all of these participants desired or saw as necessary for managing credit cards responsibly do not come naturally. So where are they supposed to learn? One of the social meanings of credit that lending circle participants pick up is that credit is synonymous with adulthood and responsibility. Unfortunately, in the United States we expect people to become responsible and acquire financial knowledge at home, or on their own. Worse yet, as the financial system grows increasingly complex, more people find it difficult to understand its intricate rules and penalties. Parents may not be able to pass along financial management skills because their own are no longer relevant to the financial realities faced by their children. Indeed, they may be facing the same challenges themselves.

For Michelle, the only preparation came the "last semester of my senior year in high school. . . . That's when I remember getting taught about finance." It proved to be too little to prepare her for being on her own. Keisha ended her interview by pointing out that while credit card companies could be found everywhere on campus, institutionalized financial education could not:

> Well, I wish that the lending circle program was on college campuses just as the credit card companies are. Even in early high school, I wish the lending circle was there to teach you how to better manage your money, how to not fall into debt. And you don't really need to fall into debt. I wish I grew up knowing that. You don't have to be in debt. You can work a minimum-wage job but live within your means, live within your budget, and I think this is a lesson that needs to be learned on a broader circle, and I wish there were more lending circles around. I really wish it was a nationwide program and especially taught in our college campuses, because some of us feel we come out of college in debt, and that's just a way of life.

Keisha's wish that lending circles be established in schools and post-secondary institutions would go a long way toward helping youth transition to adulthood with greater financial security. It would equip young people with a set of skills that would help them better navigate a complex system whose current rules are opaque. It would also begin transforming the financial service sector by negatively sanctioning costly "unofficial practices" in official settings.

Instead, too many people receive their financial education through trial and error. Among our interview participants, for example, many had had negative experiences with payday lenders, and many more had friends or family who had had negative experiences with payday lenders. These lenders' astronomical interest rates—sometimes exceeding 400 or 500 percent—had made them swear off any use of their services in the future. But many individuals have few options when they need access to as little as $400. Those who do acquire a financial education often do so too late, and in an unforgiving environment—that is, after their credit scores have plunged, their debt has accumulated, and the mainstream financial system has labeled them a failure. At the same time, the financial system has not offered many affordable alternatives for those needing to access money quickly.

Mistrust of the Financial System

Another step toward financial visibility is the opening of checking and savings accounts at established banks. Lending circle participants are required to have a checking account; the loan they receive is direct-deposited into that account, and when it is time for repayment, the

Mission Asset Fund withdraws from the account. Participants may also be encouraged to set up online payment for various services, such as utilities and phone carriers, so that monthly payments are made on time without risk of penalty.

"Unbanked" is a term often used to describe those without connections to mainstream deposit-taking institutions. In 2009, the first year for which national estimates are available, an estimated 9 million households, or roughly 8 percent of U.S. households, were unbanked.[5] These households were more likely to be nonwhite, lower income, and less educated than ones that used banks. A commonly cited reason for not having a checking or savings account is not having enough money to warrant opening one, but policymakers have become concerned that, without such accounts, families use services such as check-cashing outlets, which charge a fee for cashing checks or paying bills.

Simply having a bank account, however, does not eliminate the risk of fees. As Lisa Servon argues, check-cashing companies are transparent about their costs, while banks are not. In fact, the customers she interviewed in a check-cashing store contended that they were saving money by not using a bank. Banks commonly impose fees for going below a minimum balance, overdrawing an account, or using an ATM.[6] Such fees can pose a barrier to banking and make it difficult for those with limited resources. Many lending circle participants who became banked (or reconnected with a bank) had been hit with fees. The way these financial institutions seemed to handle their money left them confused and sometimes feeling as though they had been taken advantage of. Some questioned the competence of their banks, while others voiced skepticism about the kind of capitalism practiced in the United States. Nonetheless, achieving their dreams required being a part of this system.

In addition to dealing with fees, participants reported a need to monitor their accounts closely because mistakes and errors happened relatively frequently. Although they were quickly punished for overdrafting or letting their account dip below a certain balance, banks that made mistakes seemingly faced no consequences. When we spoke to her, Yasmeen had recently switched banks because her previous bank had not credited her account on several occasions after she made deposits. The bank's claim that it was a "data entry error" greatly concerned her. As she noted, "I'm thinking, like, what else could happen?" Maya has also switched banks because, as she claimed, "I was missing money all the time." Rosa had set up automatic payments from her checking account but reported that several bills had gone unpaid.

Facing hidden fees and charges in addition to these "errors," these participants felt as though they did not have complete control over their own money. Having a bank account, we are told, is the responsible thing to do and is allegedly the rational alternative to using high-cost financial services. Yet banks themselves may act irresponsibly, either with an individual account holder's money (or with false accounts, such as those set up by Wells Fargo employees) or with the nation's economy, as was the case in the Great Recession.

The larger financial system, of which banks are only a part, is even more complicated. MAF tries to demystify some of the complexity through its educational offerings. Jim, who was trying to clean up his credit so that he could purchase a home, said that the classes helped, but overall he found it "strange" how the financial system worked. Before coming to MAF, Keisha had been trying to get out from under the credit card debt she had accumulated in college. Initially, she had attempted to do this on her own, but she ended up paying a credit repair agency several hundred dollars per month for assistance because the entire ordeal was too confusing. As she explained:

> I did have the loan originally with Capital One, but Capital One sold the loan to someone else. So when I made an agreement to pay, whomever I was talking on the phone to was not the original [creditor] of the loan. And then another [creditor] would contact me. And listening to [National Public Radio], I realized sometimes [someone] bought the loan for pennies on the dollar. So they'll tell me I owe them something like $2,000, and they'll want me to settle. "You can pay eight hundred and something dollars right now or pay this amount in two payments," . . . and then they wanted to go into your checking account and take the monthly payments. Something didn't seem right about it, but by the time someone else called me for the same thing, I realized, okay, I have a bigger problem here. . . . To think it was an easy fix, fixing your credit, and it's not that easy at all, at all.

What Keisha is describing here is debt-buying. When people owe money, the creditor may send the bill to collections, which can be either an in-house department of the company or an outside firm under contract to collect past charges due. After going some time without collecting, the creditor may write off the debt or the debt may be sold on the market, as Keisha noted, for "pennies on the dollar." A 2014 *New York Times* article refers to the debt-buying marketplace as "often lawless" and points out that consumer information is sometimes stolen and unscrupulous debt buyers may pressure for payment on debts that have long since disappeared from an actual credit report.[7] We do not know whether this was the case for Keisha, but her story illustrates the complexity of fixing credit and highlights possibly questionable or illegal practices.

Some participants viewed the larger financial system with great skepticism. Mike knew that in order to boost his credit score, he would need to "open up a couple more lines of credit and get active with it." Nonetheless, he voiced some discomfort at doing so because "you've got to buy stuff," and he disliked this aspect of a consumer-driven capitalist system. As he pointed out, "It's a lot of games to be played" before he could increase his credit score.

Mike was not the only person who found it difficult to "play along" with this game. Mauricio, an artist, had had some success in the field but was now finding it difficult to make ends meet on his income. His wife worked, but they ended up declaring bankruptcy. The couple's financial struggles had come to a head when they tried their hand at purchasing properties for investment purposes. They ended up losing not only their investment properties but also their own home to foreclosure. Mauricio thought of the banks and the larger financial system as one big game, a rigged one whose rules he did not know:

> I think this mortgage thing is like a game. It is to me, you must know how to do it, otherwise you lose. We have made that mistake before, we have lost precisely because we don't know how to do it, because you have to know how to do it. There are a lot of people who are experts on that, especially investors. They wait, wait, save their money, and then when everything is down, they buy it. Then when it goes up, they start selling. They're the only ones, and for that you have to know, you have to know. And if you're normal, someone normal, you go to buy your house and then, if God allows it, you will get to finish paying it. Otherwise, I don't think so, unless you have good, good big businesses that allow you to pay it quickly.

He concluded his story with the remark, "That's how the system is made, well calculated." Ordinary people like him were simply "slaves" to capitalism.

Our definition of financial citizenship stresses the elimination of practices that take advantage of consumers. This means not only increasing the transparency of banking rules, rethinking the purpose of fees and hidden charges, and increasing the accountability of financial institutions, but also interrogating some of the fundamental norms and practices in the marketplace. In the current environment, however, lending circle participants faced becoming targets for exploitation because consumer protections are few.

Immigrant Invisibility

Rosa, employed in a social service agency, recounted her experience trying to secure a credit card with a national big-box store. Her application was declined because of her low credit score. "How is it possible that you can't open it for a simple number?" she exclaimed. "I showed them what I earn. I can pay for [the purchases]." That her actual financial situation might not matter was a source of bewilderment. "I was doing well with this job," she argued. "Economically, I could sustain in this country and save. However, the bank wouldn't see that, they would notice other things and refuse higher credit lines."

Daniel, an immigrant from Honduras, equated his treatment by financial institutions to the labor market's assessment of his academic credentials. College-educated, he was self-employed as a house cleaner since his course work in economics apparently counted for nothing. As he observed, "I came here and started at zero."

Stories of people who were physicians in their home countries but janitors when they came to the United States are often used to illustrate the pluck and determination of exemplary immigrants, who, according to this narrative, are willing to do whatever it takes to make it in this country. But they also illustrate how immigrants can become invisible as their past achievements are rendered worthless.[8]

Daniel's lack of a credit score made him credit-unworthy. It didn't matter that his business was doing well. He could get neither a credit card nor a loan from a car dealership. He reflected on this: "It's very different here in this country than mine. Because in my country, credit isn't important. What's important is the money. But not here."

In the United States, access to cash is not unimportant. Consider the families interviewed by Kathryn Edin and Luke Shaefer for their book *Two Dollars a Day: Living on Almost Nothing in America*. Unable to find stable employment or to access public cash welfare benefits in the wake of the 1996 welfare reform, the people they interviewed were struggling to meet their basic needs on a level of income—two dollars per person per day— that is frequently used as a measure of poverty in countries with a low gross domestic product. Without cash from paychecks or public assistance, paying rent, keeping the lights turned on, and purchasing other essential everyday items becomes challenging, if not impossible.[9]

But as lending circle participants observed, simply having cash is also not enough, since cash and credit are not interchangeable. Stable earnings may be insufficient to establish credit, particularly for those who are self-employed or paid "off the books."[10] Moreover, credit card companies sometimes require that an applicant have a Social Security number before they will issue a card. A credit history in another country is not transferrable to credit reporting agencies in the United States. On the flip side, access to and use of credit by those with no means of paying balances can lead to debt.

Some participants, both immigrant and native-born, have continued to struggle with the intricacies of the system. Bina's experience was perhaps the most ironic. She began by stating, "I'm an immigrant, so I didn't have very good credit history here in the U.S." Bina's background lies in finance, and she came to the United States to seek work in that sector. She considered herself frugal and estimated that, after paying her rent, she often spent only $100 per month on other expenses. At one point, she was working for American Express, one of the largest issuers of credit cards. Despite having a job with a high salary, Bina said that "by the time I quit Amex, I still couldn't get myself an Amex card." Her credit score was simply not high enough for the company to consider her "worthy" of its card. Through the lending circle, Bina hoped that her credit would rise and that she would finally be recognized as the contributing adult that she was.

Immigrants to the United States are expected to adapt to a certain degree to the country's practices and customs. Held out to them is the promise of a shot at the "American Dream." Yet, despite working hard, saving money, and otherwise contributing economically, many newcomers are denied one of the fundamental tools for achieving that dream, namely, access to credit.

OPENING DOORS OR SLAMMING THEM SHUT?

Despite their past bad experiences with credit cards and banks and lingering mistrust of the larger financial system, lending circle participants shared a strong desire to achieve the mantle of adulthood and visibility as they realized that good credit could lead to more opportunity. We asked all of our interviewees how they felt after learning their credit scores. An exchange between Marlene, who conducted the interviews, and Angela, a Philippine immigrant, illustrates their reaction:

MARLENE: After seeing your credit score recently, how did you feel?

ANGELA: Obsessed to have a higher credit score.

MARLENE: Why is that?

ANGELA: I think just thinking that maybe if it's higher, it's going to serve me more benefit when I go in to seek a mortgage, or making all of these large purchases, because we're also thinking of maybe getting a car.

A mortgage and a car—two symbols of the American Dream. Despite the proliferation of foreclosures caused by the housing bubble burst and

the Great Recession and the declining homeownership rates that followed these events, most non-homeowners still expect to purchase
a home in the next ten years or sooner.[11] They will most likely need good
credit to realize those expectations. Banks have been offering fewer
consumer loans in the years since the Great Recession.[12] The days of
granting mortgages without proof of income and other documentation
of payment ability—the "no-doc" or "low-doc" mortgages offered in the
years leading up to the housing crisis—are largely over. A good credit
score, then, is part of the American Dream package.

Homeownership has many benefits. For most Americans, equity in
a home is the single largest source of family wealth. Owning a home
also offers stability and a place and community where one can set down
roots. Homeownership is even associated with better health.[13] Yet for
households with lower incomes, owning a home may have downsides.
Persistent residential segregation keeps the homes affordable to lower-
income families situated in neighborhoods where values are either not
rising or not rising as quickly as elsewhere, stalling potential wealth-
building opportunities. Homeownership can thus trap people in declining areas.[14] Residential segregation was less of an issue, however, for
lending circle participants; their challenge was simply getting a foot in
the housing market.

Priced Out

A number of lending circle participants did have the goal of buying a home,
whether in the near future or later. But housing prices in the San Francisco
Bay area are among the highest in the nation. According to Trulia, a real
estate website, the 2016 median sale price for homes within the city of
San Francisco was close to or above $1 million. Across the bay in Oakland
and in other parts of the metropolitan area, prices are lower on average (the
median in these areas was $635,000 in 2016) but may still be daunting for a
household earning about $50,000 a year.[15]

Urban areas across the country are seeing steep increases in the cost
of housing, whether buying or renting. Along with San Francisco, the
cities of New York, Seattle, and Washington, D.C., have all become
extremely desirable; lower-income residents find themselves priced out
of these housing markets and forced to move outside the city. Indeed,
buying a home might require not only living outside of San Francisco
but leaving the region altogether. For example, Victor, who was saving money toward a down payment on a house, lived outside of San
Francisco in an apartment he shared with his wife, their son, his brother
in-law, and a nephew. When asked where he might purchase, he replied:

"Somewhere I can afford it, because the cost of living here is really high, so I'm going to have to move out." "Out" meant several hours away. Another example was Juan, who, like Victor, hoped to buy a house within the next two years. He was looking in Fresno, four hours southeast of San Francisco.

Good credit alone is of limited value when it comes to achieving the dream of homeownership. Neither Victor nor Juan had particularly well-paying jobs. Victor drove for a ride-hailing service, and Juan was a cook in a hotel. Juan was paying his aunt $500 a month as rent to stay in her house. As he remarked, she was "cutting him a break." But even with a move to a lower-cost area, he would have a difficult time finding a home with a mortgage payment that low. Furthermore, a monthly mortgage payment is just one cost associated with homeownership; property taxes and unexpected repair bills can place considerable strain on the budgets of many lower-income homeowners.[16]

Student Loans

Another strain on budgets, and a barrier to achieving dreams, is debt, particularly student loan debt. Credit card debt can be chipped away at with steady payments or by working out payment plans with creditors, but student loans are more daunting. The amount of these loans can be staggering. Maria had $70,000 in student loans. Her income was low enough to qualify her for a forbearance, which allows loan holders to stop making payments temporarily or to reduce their monthly payments (although interest may still accrue).[17] But forbearance, as Maria noted, does not last forever. Maria admitted that her loan "hurts like hell," but all she could do was work and make payments.

After mortgages, student loans are the largest source of debt in the United States. According to the Institute for College Access and Success, nearly 70 percent of graduating seniors in 2015 had student loan debt, averaging just over $30,000.[18] Repayment may take anywhere from ten to twenty-five years, so that by the time borrowers finish paying off their loan, they have spent far more than the initial debt. In addition, there is no way out of payment. Student loan debt is rarely included in bankruptcy filings. When asked about her greatest financial concern, one participant, Janelle, spoke about her student loan and how it would always stay with her:

> I actually only have one [loan], and it worries me because I got it in—I received the student loans not knowing that there is no way you can relieve them, you know, during—what's it called? You just have to basically pay

them off. There is no way that you can file bankruptcy or anything. So they've
been increasing, and so that's one of my biggest [concerns].

Failure to make payments, as Janelle learned, can send a credit score
spiraling downward. Thinking that the loans were in her parents'
name and that they were making payments, she did nothing for two or
three years. When that turned out not to be the case, she went into
default, and her income tax refund was garnished.

Even when student loan debt is not harming a debtor's credit score, it
is stressful. Dora, a recent college graduate, worried that she would never
find a job with a salary high enough to allow her to make good on the
numerous student loans she had taken on. She knew that the interest rates
on her loans were not high, but all the same, as she pointed out, "it is a lot
of debt." Six months after graduation, Dora had yet to find a job. Although
she could say, "My credit [score is] pretty good actually, it's not that bad,"
her improved credit was not going to eliminate the heavy burden of debt.

Homeownership is supposed to help families accumulate wealth,
and a college degree has long been the pathway to upward mobility
and increased earnings. Yet for people of color, and particularly African
Americans and Latinx, these pathways to economic stability may not
function as such.[19] Rather than an asset for the future and a ticket to a
better job, purchasing a home—if a family can even afford to do so—may
be a perilous investment and come with a high risk of foreclosure, or at
best, with limited appreciation in value if it is located in a segregated
neighborhood. The return on an investment in an advanced degree can
be difficult to foresee if the jobs one gets out of college pay relatively little
and student loan payments loom large. As Dora pointed out, having such
debt may not have a negative effect on a credit score, but it can still be
emotionally draining and difficult to get out from under. Better credit
scores, then, can open up some opportunities, but those opportunities
may still come with costs that a higher score will not ameliorate.

PUTTING FAMILY FIRST

The financial goals of lending circle participants were often intertwined
with hopes for a better life for their families. Yet here too, tensions existed.
Family members could be simultaneously a source of strain and a source
of motivation. Family members might inadvertently sabotage one family
member's efforts to be fiscally responsible and adhere to a budget. And
even if struggling, that family member perceived as financially stable
might be expected to help out the rest of the family. Moreover, even those
who lack financial resources want to be good parents and to be able to treat

their children to "extras." Participants had many different strategies for handling these tensions, all of which illustrate the inherently social nature of becoming creditworthy.

Little Acts of Sabotage

When finances are tight, we are told to "stick to a budget," usually by watching expenditures, cutting back on inessential items, and finding lower-cost alternatives for necessary items. Lending circle participants discussed their strategies for managing their budgets and watching their finances, but most did not have complete control over their money or consumption patterns. They were members of families and households in which not everyone shared the same financial goal or used the same method of arriving at it.

For some households, food appeared to be a particularly contentious point. Participants talked about ways in which they had changed their grocery shopping habits and cut back on or eliminated eating out—all in the hope of saving money and becoming more responsible. However, something as seemingly minor as a gallon of milk could become a sore spot, as Jim revealed:

> Yeah, just for dinner. I mean, I don't know what [my kids are] doing with the milk, but last week, they drank three gallons of milk, and I was like, "Really?" My wife's like, "It's nutritious. You just worry about the money." And I'm like, "Somebody's got to be worried about the money. You're not." So we often argue about that, but we're okay.

According to the U.S. Bureau of Labor Statistics, the average cost of a gallon of milk in 2016 was $3.20.[20] This may not seem like a lot of money, but at that price three gallons per week over the course of a month amounts to just under $40. For someone like Jim, who was trying to support a family of five on his salary as a cable television technician while saving up for a house, that $40 was precious. Jim also noted that his wife went out for coffee every day and that her "impulse" purchases were not helping him meet his goal of buying a home. The various little costs added up and weighed heavily on him.

Perla was equally frustrated by her partner's food consumption habits. As she tried to rein in her family's spending, her husband would

> go and buy food, especially food, how he just splurges on food! He'll buy organic, the highest-quality food, and it's like, "Oh, $150 in a day!" And the next day, "Oh, $75." It's like, well, if that's every day, oh my God, how much

are we spending? But he doesn't care. He'll just buy and then just go, "Oh, I'm going to go to Whole Foods. I'm going to go buy milk," and we buy the organic milk.

Perla was laughing as she told this story, but she was still recovering financially and emotionally from the foreclosure of not one but two homes. She proudly noted that her credit score had once been 813, at the top of the range. Even though her life was improving financially, the burden of repairing the couple's credit was falling primarily on her shoulders.

Family Expectations

Many of the immigrants we interviewed routinely sent money back home to family members or offered other types of financial assistance to relatives living outside the United States. At one point, Manuela took a second job for the sole purpose of being able to use that paycheck as remittance for her mother. Getting a credit card freed her of the need to work two jobs, as she could shift payment of her monthly bills to her card and use the cash in her checking account to help her mother. At the time of her interview, she was trying to dig herself out of the credit card debt that she had accumulated, but forgoing remittance payments was not an option. "I've always given my mother the most that I can," she explained. Bina, a young single woman, stated matter-of-factly: "I support my family; they don't support me. I have a sister here in the U.S. I support her all the time. In fact, I've gotten her a supplementary credit card based on my credit history, and anytime she needs money, I transfer it." Along with rent and utilities, financial assistance for family members was an expected monthly expense that individuals would not consider eliminating from their budgets.

One family member's ability to play the role of provider, however, may signal to others that they have no financial obligations. Manuela noted that because she lived in the United States and sent money home, her siblings placed what might have been a collective financial obligation solely on her shoulders. She told us that when her mother became ill,

I spoke with my siblings so that we could cover her costs. And, well, we're six. And my sister, I have a sister that's very sick. She didn't put in anything. The other that's more or less well, she said that she was going to try to put some in. Another said no. Another, yes. They all let the ball drop. In the end, well, I'm always the one helping. And, well, they say that when they can, they'll give and when they can't, no, although I have an agreement with them. But, well, no, they haven't respected it.

This incident put so much strain on Manuela's relationship with her siblings, she said, that she was now trying to distance herself from them.

Having access to credit can also put strain on family ties. Miki, for example, admitted that finances and money were a major source of stress and arguments with her husband. She made more money than he did and believed that she was more fiscally responsible. "We basically have separate finances," she told us, but when unexpected expenses arose on his end, she was the one who provided the funds, often on credit. Her most recent credit card debt, she explained, was the result of costs associated with her husband's travel to a relative's funeral as well as repairs he needed for his car. Being "in control" of her debt was important to Miki; as a result, she had placed her husband on a plan to repay the money she had spent on him, thus trying to ensure that she would not overextend herself. Such actions, however, can have serious consequences for a relationship. As Miki herself noted, after asking other family members to repay money that she had loaned them, they stopped speaking to her.

Children

In general, children hold a special place for their parents. Even parents with low incomes do not want their offspring to go without, and it can be difficult for them to exercise restraint when it comes to expenditures associated with their children. Events such as birthdays and graduations, impulse purchases, and big-ticket items such as college tuition are therefore common topics of conversations among those facing financial challenges. An extensive literature has documented the difficulties faced by poor and low-income families who try to provide their children with what they perceive to be a "normal" childhood.[21] But how can one reconcile this kind of spending with the goal of improving one's financial standing?

Among those we interviewed, Cynthia recounted such a challenge. "After getting a credit score of 700, I got all these offers. It was Christmastime. My youngest son was home with me visiting, and we went to all the stores, and I just let him go buy so many things off the credit cards, and I took him. And so I went crazy." Similarly, Manuela admitted that when she had extra money, she spent it on her daughter: "I like to buy a lot of things for my daughter. It's not so much for me but for my daughter. For example, if she likes some shoes, if I like them, I buy them. I spend it in that way. My son says that I'm a—how do you say it? A compulsive buyer."

But Manuela's "compulsiveness" was limited to purchases for her daughter. She was a frugal grocery shopper, buying food at a discount store and rationing the soap and shampoo used by her family. Rosa, whom we met earlier, also had difficulty curbing expenditures on her children.

A single mother and low-paid child care worker, Rosa had been participating in lending circles for several years. She had not yet received her social loan for the current circle but said that she planned to use the money to buy tablets, shoes, and clothing for her two children. She reported that the first time she participated in a lending circle, she had felt "dazzled":

> I bought [my son] an Xbox that cost $500 or $600. I think that was first. And with the rest we went out to eat that day, the twenty-fourth. We went out to eat, and we went shopping. I always like to buy them clothes in December. Although at times they tell me, "No, Mom, don't spend the money." But I like to spend the money because I feel good using it on my children.

Cynthia, a fifty-year-old with adult children, had not been able to provide gifts such as these when her children were younger. She was a recovering substance abuser, and her children had been removed from her care for a while. Although they were now successful professionals, earning enough for Cynthia to describe them as "well off," she was still trying to make up for what she perceived to be her failings as a parent. "I'm always trying to please them," she told us. So if they wanted something, she bought it, even though her desire to "please them" was contributing to her hefty credit card debt.

These lower-income mothers' use of words such as "crazy" and "compulsive" signaled their fear that they were making poor moral decisions, but spending money on their children was also a way to help their children experience "normal" childhoods while boosting their own self-esteem and sense of worth. For Cynthia, being able to spend money on her now-grown children helped assuage the guilt she felt for not having been there for them when they were young.

Those with older children also held fast to the norm that parents should help pay for their higher education. Although most participants had incomes low enough to allow their children to qualify for financial aid, this aid was not always sufficient to cover all expenses. And undocumented students, of course, are ineligible for financial aid.

Alma's daughter, for example, was about to start a study-abroad program, and her living expenses were not covered by her financial aid package. Thus, as Alma explained, "Whatever she needs, I have to supply. For example, she is going to be doing an internship this year . . . but it's an internship that requires her to move . . . and it's going to be for a year, and for the first six months of it, she will have to pay for her own tuition, for her own expenses." Alma's sole source of income was a monthly disability check. She had debt collectors calling her, and she sometimes used payday lenders to pay her bills, but, she insisted, her daughter came first; "I don't drink, I don't smoke. I think there's only rent and food and utilities. Those are my priorities. And my daughter, on top of all of that."

The right to belong is a central tenet of financial citizenship. Although Alma earned so little and owed so much, we do not suggest that she realign her priorities, nor do we believe that she was not taking to heart the financial lessons she learned at Mission Asset Fund. Yet we acknowledge that honoring individuals' choices can be challenging when funds are limited. Similarly, the challenges faced by lending circle participants, their ambivalence toward the financial system, and their continued expenditures on family should not be taken as an indication of program failure. There are many factors that lie beyond the control of both participants and the Mission Asset Fund. Unaffordable housing, student loan debt, and precarious employment are major structural challenges that face the nation and require considerable political will to solve. Despite certain legislative changes since the Great Recession, a more focused effort on the role of the financial sector seems prudent.

In our concluding chapter, we suggest policy reforms that could enhance protection for consumers and help people such as those participating in lending circles. Furthermore, these types of reforms could reframe the social meanings that people attach to credit and the financial system, shifting some power to the individual and away from credit card companies, banks, and other financial institutions that are viewed as predatory, incompetent, or even ruthless. All the same, managing finances, increasing credit scores, and getting debts under control should not have to come at the expense of family. Individuals are embedded in networks; any expectation that their obligations to members of these networks or their desire to provide for their children be set aside in the quest for a prime credit score is both unrealistic and antithetical to their right to make their own choices and pursue dignity and a sense of belonging. In short, their various experiences with credit challenge us to reflect on what it means to achieve financial citizenship in a nation where other forms of inequality are so pervasive.

Chapter 5 | Conclusion: What We Must Do

FINANCIAL CITIZENSHIP IS often deferred by a bevy of *buts*: "I'm all for a fair (or inclusive) economy . . . *but* consumers should learn how to protect themselves . . . *but* people shouldn't live beyond their means . . . *but* everyone should save today so that they don't have to suffer tomorrow." On their face, the *buts* are not entirely unreasonable as stand-alone recommendations; however, in the context of economic justice, they function as powerful disclaimers that provide cover for well-intentioned people asserting that individual consumers get themselves into financial trouble through weak will, ignorance, irresponsibility, or worse. ("It has nothing to do with race," they say, even if disadvantages are racially patterned. "It has everything to do with personal responsibility.") Their qualifications unfairly depict the exploited as authors of their own fates who unwisely seek out or succumb to the appeal of products and services that they do not need. According to this view, not everyone deserves financial citizenship, and any attempt to impose it universally would reward unworthy individuals engaged in bad behavior, while endangering the diligent. In short, this view insists on whitewashing the chapters of history that make today's inequalities more durable.

These ahistorical concerns about individual behavior may hold up when looking at any one individual, whether that person is "splurging" on organic groceries or on their children's school clothes, obtaining a high-cost payday loan to fix a broken-down car or to catch up on a past-due mobile phone account, making a costly withdrawal from a retirement savings account to pay for routine expenses, or acquiring a pricey subprime mortgage for a slowly appreciating property at high risk of foreclosure. It is easier to lament such decisions, pointing out that the person should have known better, than it is to acknowledge that other actors and institutions encouraged these decisions or even made them necessary.

Individual behaviors did not create these patterns of economic injustice, so an individual's self-reform cannot change those patterns without assistance. Let's consider what self-reform might look like and why it remains inadequate as a response to economic inequality. According to William Darity and Darrick Hamilton, the family of an African American with a college degree has less wealth than the family of a white person who has not finished high school. The black family's lack of wealth does not result from failing to save money; they do save, but they also extend assistance to family and community.[1] Nor is it a consequence of underinvesting in education; black families overinvest in education compared with their white counterparts. Many black families have followed the recommendations for saving and investing, but they cannot as individuals close a gap that is structural. To say that there is a structural gap is to acknowledge that wealth (and its opposite) are built up and passed along from generation to generation. These patterns harden and widen over time as yesterday's disadvantage makes tomorrow's advancement more difficult. Over time the accumulation of disadvantage comes to be seen as "natural," as an outcome of individual preferences and capacities independent of the policy histories that lowered the returns on investment for education, housing, work, and asset accumulation for communities of color and others (see chapter 2).

Ignoring these histories of disadvantage falsely equates the more powerful exploiter with those he exploits. It is like proposing that we fix domestic violence by asking that a survivor get educated about her condition without sanctioning her abuser. Focusing on the abuser does not negate the value of coaching or other supports for the survivor. It simply places the lion's share of the blame where it belongs and opens the door to a more therapeutic approach to the survivor's security. The abuser can be punished, and potential abusers can be regulated into less damaging behavior. Questions can also be asked about why the abused is in such close proximity to (and therefore more likely to select) such dangerous partners. At the same time, the survivor can help craft a new approach to partner selection and to forging a safer way to meet and maintain new partnerships. As with love, so too with finance.

Just as romantic relationships can be toxic, unfair economic arrangements can corrode the safety and self-regard of individuals, their loved ones, and their communities. In *Toxic Inequality*, Thomas Shapiro argues that wealth inequality is not merely a material condition but also a pernicious force when mixed with shifting racial and ethnic demographics and with the hidden advantages of race that allow individuals to pretend that their well-being results solely from their own grit, discipline, and individual sacrifice. This perspective justifies the view that the economic problems of others come from sloth, weak will, and out-of-control desires.

Regrettably, in this toxic cocktail of conditions, dismissing individual responsibility as the fundamental factor driving inequality may be perceived as belittling the struggles of those who took their meager talents and, with difficulty, made more.

Under these circumstances, what can be done? Our call to action begins with a few guiding principles based on a definition of financial citizenship and the ways in which the proposed changes to policies and programs could affect the experience of dignity, respect, and fairness in people's daily lives. These principles look to both large-scale policy changes and the individual behaviors and programs targeting them that can contribute to a more just economic existence for all.

GUIDING PRINCIPLES

The guiding principles we propose are based on a definition of financial citizenship as: the bundle of rights that people sense that they deserve vis-à-vis the financial sector's reach into their private lives. These social rights take into account how consumer credit scoring and financial services have become consequential for dignity, respect, autonomy, and belonging. These guiding principles push us beyond changing the behavior of individuals and toward acknowledging the histories that have generated inequality and honoring what individuals and communities are already doing to confront disadvantage. Indeed, when making financial decisions, individuals are taking others into account and responding to conditions that existed long before they did. After articulating these principles, we turn to some illustrative policies and programs that could help usher in an era of widespread financial citizenship.

1. *We must recognize that conscious policy choices are responsible for our existing inequalities and that it will take clearly intentioned policies to undo their impact.* It is far easier to resort to a few stylized facts than to confront the complexities of history. Yet a few facts help us navigate the messiness of history. Darity and Hamilton argue that racial inequalities persist because once blacks and Latinx were finally able to buy homes, they did so in neighborhoods where houses appreciated at much slower rates than houses appreciate for whites. Moreover, when people of color were finally free to attend any universities they wanted, they usually went to them from underresourced high schools and entered majors and social networks that did not give them the same return on their investment as happened with their white counterparts. Blacks' entry into the mainstream marketplace thus came late in the game, and when they were financially disadvantaged. The expectation that

they should still manage to achieve financial equality has been met in only relatively few anomalous cases.[2] Closing the opportunity gap for people of color would therefore entail not only their hard work but a substantial transfer of resources by the state and the private sector.

2. *We must tackle exploitation.* If we are to take the right to freedom from exploitation seriously, we must confront exploiters. The challenge here is sorting them out: financial service providers seldom play the stock characters of the villain or the hero; indeed, some take on both roles— helping with one hand while hurting with the other. Some forms of exploitation are clearly illegal (such as opening a costly bank account without a customer's consent), but most are not. The latter include high-cost loans designed to ensnare consumers with balloon payments or unclear terms that land them in debt traps. Just as credit scoring agencies can predict which consumers are most likely to default, so too we have a right to know which financial service providers are likeliest to entice consumers into downward debt spirals. And just as a store is not allowed to sell products with malfunctions that could severely harm consumers, so too regulatory restrictions should be placed on financial service providers whose products come with unrecognized malfunctions or shrewdly designed dangers.[3]

3. *We must move away from targeting the individual and instead target the relationships that matter most to them.* We have demonstrated that by and large individuals do not fall into debt owing to frivolous expenses; nor do they weigh their financial choices in a vacuum. Instead, they use financial services to manage the needs and priorities of loved ones. Thus, rather than start with a specific sum of money (the budget constraint), it would be better to look at the individual's web of relationships and what these require to be maintained. Parents want their children to have experiences comparable to those of their peers, and children want their parents to be comfortable in old age and to be able to meet death with dignity. When participating in the life of their communities, individuals also want control in order to demonstrate that they have the power to give a little and save a little while attending to the necessities of food and shelter. In the most literal sense, they do not live for bread (or shelter or money) alone.

4. *The emphasis on dying with dignity in public health should be extended to living with dignity.* Regardless of their backgrounds, individuals try to pursue their vision of a good life—a vision generally shared by other members of their community—and to do so with dignity. In other words, while affirming their right to self-determination and social belonging, they are also trying to evade affronts to their dignity. Typically, such affronts

are directed at parents, members of faith communities, or caretakers for parents living on inadequate retirement funds. Individuals are willing to take on costly debts to avoid the shame of being unable to offer a child a costly graduation party (costly in that it adds another expense to an already overstretched budget) or to bury a family member in a manner deemed appropriate by their community. Moreover, when they are willing to acquire debt to deal with short-term liquidity needs, individuals sometimes try to avoid situations that cause them embarrassment. (Why go to a bank and risk being the object of disparaging remarks when payday lenders treat everyone well?) Instead of portraying costly financial decisions as manifestations of a "lack" of education or self-control (as deficit models), we should focus on the strategies and priorities that individuals adopt to affirm their own dignity (and that of their loved ones) and shield it from affronts.

5.   *Product design should come from its intended users.* Even well-designed goods can cause harm when their design is based exclusively on the needs and experiences of the ideal middle-class consumer. This imagined consumer does not have a volatile income, but even if she does, she does not expect a financial service to be fraught with encounters that engender embarrassment, shame, or downright humiliation. When it comes to finances, as with everything else, not everyone is socialized in the same way. Whether and how to speak about finances, and what to do when one's financial situation takes a decidedly negative turn, differ from community to community and from one individual to the next. Rather than change how people are socialized so that they too can use the products and services tailored to meet the needs of the financially comfortable, we propose that products be designed based on what borrowers already do with their money. We would also expand the pool of consumers we imagine as using financial services to include those not usually prioritized by mainstream banks, namely, those who earn low or irregular income and thus are accustomed to frequent transactions. In other words, how could financial products and services be codesigned with this newly prioritized group of users, who have been disproportionately harmed by the current assortment of financial options?

ADVANCING FINANCIAL CITIZENSHIP: KEY POLICIES AND PROGRAMS

We begin with examples of policies and programs that could transform people's experience of financial services and social belonging. Can we imagine a world where financial products and services are assessed according to whether they affirm a right to be free from exploitation and a right to dignity-enhancing experiences? What if individuals and communities had a voice in the design and rollout of financial products and services? How could the consumers of these financial services also operate as coproducers of financial culture? We conclude with a discussion of ways to secure seed capital for every child (a more market-oriented approach to baby bonds) and provide short-term loans to all who need them without dragging them into a debt spiral. The following policies and programs are not exhaustive, but they do represent a range of activities that could advance financial freedoms—freedom from exploitation, freedom to be recognized and respected, and freedom to experience social belonging— while allowing those who use them to be cocreators of culture.

Seed Capital for Every Child ("Baby Bonds")

Blacks and Latinx will never be able to catch up with their white counterparts simply by working at the same jobs, engaging in the same savings and investment practices, or getting the same education. Historical records show that, on average, whites inherit over ten times as much wealth as do blacks and Latinx—*by design*. Even if inheritance is disregarded, people of color tend to purchase their nest-egg home in neighborhoods where houses appreciate more slowly than houses do in other neighborhoods. Furthermore, holding other things equal, people of color do not benefit as much as their white counterparts from social networks formed at universities.

We are calling for seed capital for every child, building on an idea proposed by Darity and Hamilton, namely, that an investment account be established for every citizen at birth and become retrievable for college expenses or for starting a business once the child reaches the age of eighteen.[4] The amount proposed by Darity and Hamilton is $60,000 for children of any race born to families with wealth below the American median. If a family has more than the median wealth, the amount of the grant would be less. Although the annual cost of such a program would top $60 billion, it is considerably less than the $100 billion in benefits granted by the 2016 tax code to people earning over $1 million.[5]

Our proposal builds on the lessons we learned at the Mission Asset Fund, where a sense of individual ownership, control, and group belonging seems to make a difference in how people experience financial products and services. We imagine a system whereby community members and private-sector groups could contribute to a child's seed capital and thus grant those helping the child achieve success a sense of ownership and pride. Contributions to the fund could take the form of ritual events that reaffirm the child's progress toward adulthood (for example, graduation from kindergarten, elementary school, or middle school and the quinceañera).[6] Rather than placing too many restrictions on how these funds could be used, we can imagine a group of young people pooling their resources to start a business, siblings working with parents to buy a franchise of a food company or retail store in which their parents are employed, or a young couple making a sizable down payment on a house with money to spare in the event of a job loss or major maintenance need. In other words, providing seed capital would be useful to the extent that young people would have the freedom to work creatively by mixing and matching resources to build opportunity and pursue meaningful lives. Some commentators have expressed concern that too much freedom might lead young people to "waste" the money or to be burdened with too many family pressures to spend it productively. In response to such concerns, we would point out that respect and freedom from exploitation are important components of financial citizenship. It is conceivable that some will not take full advantage of these new opportunities; nevertheless, such opportunities will send to coming generations an important message and a roadmap to financial citizenship.

Short-Term Loans for Every Family

Earnings today are not as steady as they used to be. Whenever income for a week or a month comes up short (that is, when it falls below the median), as it does for about three months out of the year in many American households, the family cannot meet its expenses in the usual way. Fluctuating earnings combined with lack of savings leave many families with few or no alternatives to costly short-term loans. We propose reducing the costs of these loans and avoiding the indignities that they can impose on those pursuing them.

In such a scenario, both the government and the private sector would offer short-term loan products. Post-office banking, for example, could compete with nonprofits and financial service companies. Just as it is possible to send express mail via UPS—a private-sector provider—so too it should be possible to obtain loans handled by post offices, banks, other for-profit companies, nonprofits, and public/private-sector hybrid providers.[7] Employers too could make visible and more easily available short-term loans to employees based on length of employment and behaviors at work indicating an individual's reliability. Such options would require bold thinking on ways to reduce regulatory barriers for loan providers, pool risks and resources, and prevent exploitation in this new marketplace, with clear regulations that manage not to overreach.

In the short term, the National Credit Union Authority (NCUA) should expand the field of competitors offering short-term loans by changing its payday alternative loan (PAL) program rules to make it more feasible for credit unions to expand their offerings of lower-cost loans. These changes would also encourage reporting to credit bureaus, ensure affordable payments, and create superior alternatives not just for those who use payday and auto title loans but also for those who currently use other forms of expensive credit, like late fees, overdraft, pawn loans, rent-to-own services, and subprime installment loans.

The very low revenue constraints under the PAL program have made this lending unprofitable. On a $500, three-month loan, credit unions can charge just $44, which is not enough to cover their costs and invest in the automation needed for this lending to grow. Payday lenders typically charge about $450 in fees to borrow $500 for three months—an exorbitant sum. Of course, the NCUA should not allow rates that are anywhere in the ballpark of payday loan rates, but allowing rates that are somewhat higher than proposed would allow small-loan programs to reach scale. Similarly, it is important that credit unions be able to offer small lines of credit. Providing loan providers with this needed flexibility through the use of safer products would go a long way toward increasing consumers' choices and their ability to ensure the well-being of their loved ones.

Finally, a variety of nonprofit organizations using the lending circles model and others using models that have not yet been formalized should be allowed to compete with both credit unions and for-profit providers. The model for this legislation is California's SB 896, which passed without opposition. The bill provides regulatory assurance for nonprofits and new opportunities for asset-building, partly through the evasion of asset-stripping products. The main components of the bill include the following:

- Declaring that nonprofit organizations have an important role to play in helping individuals obtain access to affordable, credit-building loans

- Granting a licensing exemption within the California Finance Lenders Law (CFLL) for 501(c)(3) nonprofits facilitating zero-interest loans of up to $2,500

- Enabling nonprofit organizations to apply for exemption to provide zero-interest loans if they meet other conditions such as providing credit education, reporting to national credit agencies, opening books to the Department of Business Oversight upon request, and annually reporting lending data to the DBO[8]

Regulating Safety for Short-Term Loans

On the one hand, consumers need more options, so the previous recommendations focused on increasing the menu of choices that promote financial well-being. On the other hand, short-term loans need more than a new set of competitors to make consumers better off; they also need regulations. The *Cincinnati Enquirer* offers a useful summary of how a new law in Ohio (a political bellwether) can make payday and other short-term loans safer for consumers:

- The monthly payment on a loan for fewer than ninety days is limited.
- The payment, including fees and repayment of the initial loan, cannot exceed 6 percent of the borrower's gross monthly income or 7 percent of the borrower's net monthly income.
- Fees and interest on loans for more than ninety days but less than one year cannot exceed 60 percent of the initial loan amount. For example, a borrower who takes out a $500 loan will not pay more than $300 in fees.
- Monthly fees are limited to 10 percent of the original loan amount or $30, whichever is less.
- Prorated fees and interest are returned to borrowers who pay off their loan early.[9]

Extending Safety Regulations to Student Loans

If we pay attention to the struggles of young people and the families supporting their education, we find that not just short-term loans but also long-term ones harm consumers. Parents and relatives take out loans or miss payments on their other bills in order to help their loved ones keep up with student loans. Because federal student loans cannot be discharged, the borrower cannot file for bankruptcy; moreover, there are few federal or private-sector opportunities to restructure education loans. Why should students bear all of the risk of pursuing higher education? If they are unable to secure the kinds of jobs that facilitate timely repayment of those loans, why not find a less burdensome route to repayment? We propose that the federal student loan program offer a fair reduction in monthly costs to those whose incomes justify it. The entire industry deserves a haircut, offering blanket forgiveness for a proportion of all outstanding loans. And we propose tighter regulation of nonfederal student loans going forward.

Dignity Assessments

It is not just the loans, the bank accounts, and the credit cards that matter; it is also how they are administered. If we recognize that every human being has a right to dignity, then we cannot view finance, banking, or welfare programs as being "dignity-neutral" or value-free. The spheres in which we pursue dignified lives are neither separate from nor hostile to those in which we take out loans, invest in retirement, or receive government assistance for food, housing, or job training and other forms of education. All of these spheres imbricate social and financial practices. Just as an assessment of environmental impact anticipates the harms that policies and programs might inflict on a particular site, so too an assessment of dignity could identify the indignities that consumers might experience when seeking, maintaining, and terminating financial services and products or when their overdue debts go to collections.

How might new programs and services increase respect for and recognition of an individual's autonomy—or even their time? What type of message is more likely to make a consumer internalize financial difficulty as a personal failing rather than externalize it as a set of circumstances to be managed? How can the delivery of products and services be mainstreamed so that low- and moderate-income people feel that they are treated as respectfully as everyone else is treated and that their children and other loved ones have a chance to be respected by virtue of having access to dignity-affirming programs and services? It is not enough to be aware of disparate material outcomes; we must also know whether the subjective experience of financial inclusion activates the core human values of dignity, respect, and a concern for fairness.

Participatory Design of Financial Products

Rather than assume that finance is too complicated and financial technologies too alien for low- and moderate-income families to understand, we believe that the principle of participatory design would help all stakeholders develop tools that make sense from the perspective of these consumers of financial products—that is, tools that acknowledge and incorporate the potential meaning of financial products and services for these users. What resonates with some audiences may not do so with others. Tools that are efficient from a technical standpoint may not be attractive to the populations they are meant to help.

Participatory design can take various forms. The Mission Asset Fund, for example, began by asking how financial providers might transform the widespread and long-standing community practice of rotating savings and credit associations into a standard, formal offering. A number of community stakeholders engaged in conversations with MAF as it designed the product and deliberately tried to describe the technical aspects of the new financial product (lending circles) in language that was easily comprehensible to its engaged audiences. This kind of design participation symbolically emphasizes community ownership by reminding people that the money is their own and by describing a lending circle as a valuable community asset that has been undervalued by outsiders. Through public-private partnerships, communities can design financial products in collaboration, gathering the voices and experiences of people who have usually been handed a product and told to use it rather than asked to help create it. Design participation is a practice that is more likely to lead to greater financial security as people pursue dignity and pay the price for belonging.

Participatory Education

Rather than view financial education as a one-way transfer of knowledge, we should think about it as participatory. Those seeking help may themselves possess strategies and rules of thumb that could be helpful to others or modified in some way to improve their own financial lives.

Financial education should also be straightforward. In *The Financial Diaries*, the researchers Jonathan Morduch and Rachel Schneider cite a study by the Urban Institute in which fourteen thousand credit union customers were given simple advice on how to use a credit card:

Don't swipe the small stuff. Use cash when it's under $20.

Credit keeps charging. It adds approximately 20% to the total.

A simple intervention like this one, the study found, in limiting advice to two rules of thumb and relaying trust that people can figure out the rest themselves, does in fact enable people to reduce debt and increase savings.[10]

Finally, financial education should be multivocal. Both children and adults other than the household head influence how a household's finances are managed. Their voices pressure heads of household to make decisions that balance the needs of and attachments to these different household members. Participatory financial education would allow families to function as their own support groups and assist those among them who are trying to reduce debt and increase financial security. What if families were to engage in budgeting as a group?[11] What if elementary and middle school students learned about saving, wealth, credit scores, and the history of financial inequality along with history, English, and math? What if talking about finances lost its stigma and consumers felt comfortable asking questions about lower-cost alternatives to services and products, knowing they would not be embarrassed or belittled for not knowing "obvious" things? In short, we are calling for an approach to financial education that respects all our various relationships that are implicated in our decisions to spend, borrow, or sacrifice.

CONCLUSION

Changes in banking and finance have made it nearly impossible for individuals and families to live outside the financial system. Given the high cost of credit invisibility or a subprime credit score and the power of both to impede an individual's full participation in society, there seems to be no alternative but to engage in the formal financial sector.[12] Without presenting the defeatist narrative of "no alternative," we have striven in this book to shed light on the financial practices that individuals use to accomplish social things. People express belonging and care and signal moral concerns in how they handle money, while doing their best to maintain their dignity in the process.

Rather than insist that consumers learn to speak the "proper" language of household finances, the language and value calculations they already use when accounting for their finances can be interpreted. Like Borges's fictional character Funes the Memorious, consumers refer to money numbers by a variety of terms: gas money, grocery money, family money, the funeral fund, emergency money, good money, and no money.[13] By taking these terms and their meanings seriously, we can better understand how people make sense of what they owe, what they need, and the nature of their priorities. Designing financial services that communicate in the vernacular will respect people's rights to indigenous language and improve their participation in family and community life.

Individual behavior certainly matters, but there are some things that lie beyond the reach of personal responsibility. The lack of intergenerational wealth among people of color is the result of government policies as well as real estate and banking practices—not undisciplined expenditure by individuals. If the call for government and private-sector accountability were to ring as loud as it does for personal grit and self-control, consumers would find themselves traversing fairer terrain. An individual's hard work and sacrifice do not pay off without assistance from the government and the private sector. Ingenuity without seed capital and tight budgets without slack get in the way of a more just economic life.

In a society that prioritizes financial citizenship, freedoms are advanced while reasonable safety is assured. Nonprofits like the Mission Asset Fund—as well as nonprofits whose models we have not yet imagined—have the freedom to identify meaningful practices that can make people's lives better. And consumers are at liberty to try new products and services and to learn by doing. We are not so naive as to believe that freedom stands without constraint; therefore, we also insist on regulations that protect people from outright exploitation and set reasonable road rules so that powerful financial engines do not rev up too quickly, speeding along highways with abandon. Liberty and restraint will remain in tension, as they should.

Financial citizenship can be realized. There are other solutions to the problems of credit, debt, and asset-building. They begin with the recognition that low- and moderate-income consumers are worthy of respect, that credit is crucial for asset-building, and that the economic crimes of the past are not past and remain predictive of our undisrupted futures. From the Mission Asset Fund, *Credit Where It's Due* has gleaned lessons in disruption and constructed blueprints for opening up more opportunities in the existing economy—an economy that is not yet inclusive. A just economy will require bold moves from above and meaningful engagements from below. It can be done.

Epilogue |

FOR A MOMENT it seemed as though they could all come out. There was no longer any need to stay invisible or serve as easy targets of exploitation. Those formerly excluded from the world of finance and politics were inching their way in. Their contributions to the economy, it seemed, would only grow, while the laws they had been forced to evade could now be reasonably honored.

The future looked promising until the Trump administration's decision to end the Deferred Action for Childhood Arrivals (DACA) on September 5, 2017. The raids began shortly thereafter. Those older adults who had voluntarily stepped out of the shadows to embrace political and financial visibility were among the first to face deportation.

Melecio Andazola Morales worked construction, paid his taxes, and kept a clean record. He had also reared four children, all U.S. citizens, including one who had earned her way into Yale. Morales checked in as required while applying for legal status on October 12, 2017. He and his daughter Viviana arrived at the Citizenship and Immigration Services (CIS) office in Centennial, Colorado, to what they thought was his final interview for a green card. Instead, he, the family's sole breadwinner, was arrested. Deportation came swiftly, on December 15, 2017.[1]

Romulo Avelica-Gonzalez drove to Lincoln Heights School, just beyond downtown Los Angeles, to drop off his eleven-year-old daughter. As he approached the next school stop with his thirteen-year-old in the backseat, an unmarked black vehicle sped ahead and blocked his way, while another penned his car from behind. After living in the United States for twenty-five years with his four daughters, all of whom are U.S. citizens, Romulo was going to jail (or "detention," as some call it). Deportation would mean an end to the income that his family needed to survive.[2]

Like Romulo, Perla Morales-Luna abruptly faced deportation. She and her two young daughters were walking down the sidewalk on their way to pay the month's rent. Suddenly three men leapt out of a U.S. Customs and Border Patrol SUV, grabbed Perla, and instructed her daughters to stay

113

back. Bereft, the girls began wailing.[3] With their mom ripped away, where did they belong?

Back in San Francisco, a young college student in school to become a nurse watched these episodes in dismay. She had used the lending circles program to pay her $495 DACA application fee. The Lending Circles for Dreamers program was meant to combine political citizenship with financial belonging. The prospect of being able to attend school without fear of being kicked out or herded up had raised her hopes of contributing to her own educational development and the well-being of her family, her community, and the nation. With DACA coming to an end, she and others began scrambling to come up with the renewal fee. If they could do so in time, they might be able to finish their studies while the politicians figured out the next step.[4]

More than a well-timed loan was needed, José Quiñonez argued, to respond to the cancellation of DACA. He understood all too well that invisibility was a condition of survival. Realizing how many young people would soon confront ruin, he and his team at Mission Asset Fund decided to raise money to offer full scholarships to cover the dreamers' renewal fees. The fund already had $50,000 set aside for DACA loans, but it went on to raise a total of $4 million that it could distribute as grants. As Quiñonez realized, "doing nothing was not an option." Although a onetime infusion of cash would not solve the problem, it could help buy more time—and afford new opportunities.

In their pursuit of a better education for their children or themselves, these Dreamers were trying to belong, and their longing to belong had to be routed through the financial system. Students were navigating the costs of tuition, shelter, and transportation, and young parents had to shoulder the routine costs of parenting—school supplies, transportation, clothes, fund-raisers, sports, birthday parties, and holiday events. How they met these financial needs signaled both to them and to others how well they were incorporated into society and how much security their loved ones could expect. Through their financial practices, they could become more visible to their loved ones, their communities, and the financial system. By contrast, the lack of citizenship rights made them feel smaller and less vibrant as they attempted not to draw attention to themselves in order to evade deportation, wage garnishments, or curtailment of the little credit they could marshal.

National citizenship and financial citizenship share a number of similarities and cannot be said to occupy separate spheres. More, they function as arenas for individuals and organizations to contest who belongs, why, and with what responsibilities and privileges. As another cycle of citizenship veers from wrangling to ruin to repair, we are at a moment threatened with reversal, or at least paralysis. Historically, social downturns have eventually swung back up, but not on their own. Social movement actors, politicians, social entrepreneurs, and socially responsible innovators have had to make it so. That struggle continues.

Photographs |

Photo 1   Ana Velazquez with Her Son, Hopeful for Their Future

Source: Photo courtesy of Mission Asset Fund.

Photo 2   Jonathan Blanco Rojas, a Dreamer, After Receiving
           a $495 Scholarship to Renew His DACA Application

Source: Photo courtesy of Mission Asset Fund.

Photo 3   After Being Featured in the *Wall Street Journal*, MAF Client
            Shweta Kohli Meets with MAF Program Staff to Continue
            Her Ascent

Source: Photo courtesy of Mission Asset Fund.

Photo 4   A Lending Circle Formation at the San Francisco
LGBT Center

Source: Photo courtesy of Mission Asset Fund.

Photo 5   Alicia in the Farmer's Market After Formally Establishing
Her Business, Alicia's Tamales Los Mayas

Source: Photo courtesy of Mission Asset Fund.

Photo 6   Flor Vaca Proudly Surveys Her Restaurant, Mr. Pollo,
           and What It Means for Her Family and Community

Source: Photo courtesy of Mission Asset Fund.

Photo 7   MAF Founder José Quiñonez Explaining His Vision for
the Lending Circles as Program Director Mohan Kanungo
(Far Right) Looks On

Source: Photo courtesy of Mission Asset Fund.

17 2 Photographs

Photo 8   Doris Vasquez Warmly Welcoming a MAF Member
to Discuss His Plans for the Future

Source: Photo courtesy of Mission Asset Fund.

Appendix A | The Interviewees

ID/Pseudonym	Age Range	Race-Ethnicity	Occupation
Maria	46–50	Latinx	Small-business owner
Dora	25 and under	Latinx	Preschool teacher
Arlene	41–45	Latinx	House cleaner
Tina	36–40	Latinx	House cleaner
Abel	51–55	Latinx	Unclear
Alberto	36–40	Latinx	Electrician
Isaac	31–35	Unspecified	Unemployed
Teresa	66 and over	Unspecified	Unemployed
Barbara	41–45	Unspecified	Unemployed
Celeste	41–45	Asian	Small-business owner
Umberto	66 and over	Latinx	Retired
Cynthia	51–55	African American	Social worker
Manuela	51–55	Latinx	Custodian
Carolina	25 and under	Latinx	Unemployed
Elliot	46–50	Asian	Accountant
Janelle	25 and under	African American	Paralegal
Lola	66 and over	Unspecified	Retired
Virginia	61–65	Unspecified	Unemployed
Olive	36–40	Asian	Uber driver
Yasmeen	36–40	Middle Eastern	Customer service/ dispatch
Josephine	61–65	African American	Uber driver
Fernando	26–30	Latinx	Social worker
David	26–30	Unspecified	Unemployed
Alphonso	41–45	Latinx	Small-business owner
Lorraine	31–35	Asian	Small-business owner
Hung	41–45	Asian	Security and landscaping
Greg	46–50	Unspecified	Senior care worker
Miki	36–40	Asian	Manager

(Table continues on p. 124)

ID/Pseudonym	Age Range	Race-Ethnicity	Occupation
Jim	36–40	Unspecified	Telecommunications technician
Perla	36–40	Asian	Paralegal
Marcela	66 and over	Latinx	Unemployed
Fabiana	41–45	Unspecified	Small-business owner
Ines	51–55	Latinx	Small-business owner
Mike	36–40	Unspecified	Social worker
Alma	61–65	Asian	Unemployed
Bina	31–35	Asian	Engineer
Keisha	46–50	Unspecified	Teacher
Marco	51–55	Latinx	Small-business owner
Alejandra	46–50	Latinx	House cleaner
Salome	31–35	Latinx	Office staff
Ramon	41–45	Latinx	Restaurant worker
Carmelo	26–30	Latinx	Restaurant manager
Alvaro	51–55	Latinx	Small-business owner
Mauricio	61–65	Latinx	Musician
Daniel	56–60	Latinx	Teacher
Maya	36–40	Latinx	Baker
Tomas	36–40	Latinx	Agricultural worker
Victor	36–40	Latinx	Small-business owner/ Uber driver
Michelle	26–30	Unspecified	Banking
Paul	31–35	Latinx	Unemployed
Angela	36–40	Asian	Unemployed
Simón	51–55	Latinx	Small-business owner
Sergio	26–30	Unspecified	Retail
Daniel	36–40	Latinx	House cleaner
Armando	41–45	Latinx	Hotel worker
Rosa	36–40	Latinx	Senior care worker
Valerie	46–50	Latinx	House cleaner

Appendix B | Mission Asset Fund Programs Application

PROGRAMS APPLICATION/ SOLICITUD DE PROGRAMAS

This information is confidential and will only be used to evaluate if you qualify for our programs./Esta información es confidencial y únicamente será utilizada para evaluar si usted califica para nuestros programas.

First name/Primer nombre: _____

Middle name/Segundo nombre: _____

Last name/Apellido: _____

Date of birth/Fecha de nacimiento:_____

Country of birth/País de nacimiento:_____

Language(s)/Idioma(s): _____

SSN/No. de Seguro Social: _____

ITIN/Número de impuestos: _____

Gender/Género: _____ Female/Femenino _____ Male/Masculino

Address/Dirección: _____

City, state/Ciudad, estado: _____

Zip code/Código postal: _____

Mailing address (*if different from above*)/Dirección de correo (*si es diferente a su casa*): _____

Email: _____

Home phone/Teléfono (hogar): _____

Cell phone/Celular: _____

Cell-phone provider/Proveedor de celular: _____

Emergency Contact: *Please provide the name and contact information of a family member or friend who would know how to reach you if you change addresses.*/**Contacto de Emergencia:** *Por favor proporcione el nombre y contacto de un familiar o amigo(a) que sabría cómo ubicarle en caso de que usted se cambie de casa.*

Name/Nombre: _____

Relationship/Relación: _____

Phone/Teléfono: _____

Address/Dirección: _____

City, state/Ciudad, estado: _____

Zip code/Código postal: _____

Employment Information/Información Laboral

Employment status *(choose one)*/Estado laboral *(escoja uno)*:

___ I work more than full-time *(more than 40 hours per week)*/Trabajo más que tiempo completo *(más de 40 horas por semana)*

___ I work full-time/Trabajo tiempo completo

___ I work part-time/Trabajo medio tiempo

___ I am self-employed/Trabajo por cuenta propia

___ I am a student and work as well/Estudio o recibo capacitación vocacional y trabajo también

___ I am a student/Soy un estudiante

___ Unemployed/Desempleado

How frequently do you get paid?/¿Con qué frecuencia le pagan?

___ Weekly/Semanalmente

___ Monthly/Mensualmente

___ Every 2 weeks/Cada 2 semanas

___ Other/Otro: _____

Payment method?/¿Forma de pago?

___ Check/Cheque

___ Direct deposit/Depósito directo

___ Cash/Efectivo

___ Other/Otro: _____

Employer or name of business/Empleador o nombre de su negocio:

_____

Position or title/Posición o título: _____

Household Information/Información de su Hogar

What's your household size?/¿De cuántas personas se compone su hogar? _____

How many adults (*over 18*) live in your home (*including you*)?/ ¿Cuántos adultos (*mayor de 18 años*) viven en su hogar (*inclúyase a usted mismo[a]*)? _____

How many children do you financially support?/¿Cuántos niños mantiene económicamente? _____

How many people in your home are working?/¿Cuántas personas en su hogar están trabajando? _____

Household Income/Ingresos de su Hogar

Please list the monthly GROSS income (before taxes) of your household/ Por favor anote el ingreso BRUTO mensual (antes de pagar impuestos) de su hogar:

Formal employment (*your salary*)/Empleo formal (*su salario*): $_____

Self-employment income/Trabajo por cuenta propia: $_____

Government assistance/Asistencia del gobierno (*TANF, food stamps/ estampillas de comida, SSI/Seguro Social, unemployment/desempleo, or veterans' benefits/beneficios para veteranos*): $_____

Pension/Jubilación: $_____

Alimony or child support/Manutención para menores, asistencia de divorcio o separación: $_____

Income from other family members/Ingresos de otros miembros familiares: $_____

Investment income/Ingreso de inversiones: $_____

Other income (*please specify*)/Otros ingresos (*favor especifique*): $_____

TOTAL: $_____

Assets and Liabilities/Bienes y Deudas

Please answer the questions below. If you answer Yes, *specify the value and corresponding debt./Por favor responda las siguientes preguntas. Si responde Sí, debe especificar valor y deuda correspondiente.*

Do you own a car?/¿Es usted dueño(a) de un (o más de un) vehículo?

___Yes/Sí ___ No

Vehicle value/Valor del vehículo: $_____

Outstanding debt/Deuda pendiente: $_____

Do you own your home?/¿Es usted dueño(a) de su casa?

___ Yes/Sí ___ No

Home value/Valor de la casa: $_____

Outstanding debt/Deuda pendiente: $_____

Do you own a business?/¿Es usted dueño(a) de un negocio?

___ Yes/Sí ___No

Business value/Valor del negocio: $_____

Outstanding debt/Deuda pendiente: $_____

Do you have investments (*IRA, mutual funds, stocks, etc.*)?/¿Tiene inversiones (*como acciones, bonos, fondos de jubilación*)?

___ Yes/Sí ___ No

Investments value/Valor inversiones: $_____

Do you have a checking account?/¿Tiene cuenta corriente (de cheques)?

___ Yes/Sí ___ No

Bank name: _____

Balance: $_____

Do you have a savings account?/¿Tiene cuenta de ahorro?

___ Yes/Sí ___ No

Bank name: _____

Balance: $_____

Do you owe money to friends or family?/¿Usted le debe dinero a amigos o familiares?

___ Yes/Sí ___ No

Amount you owe/Cantidad que debe: $_____

Do you have an outstanding credit card balance?/¿Tiene un saldo pendiente en su(s) tarjeta(s) de crédito?

___ Yes/Sí ___ No

Amount you owe/Cantidad que debe: $_____

Do you have student loans?/¿Debe usted préstamos estudiantiles?

___ Yes/Sí ___ No

Amount you owe/Cantidad que debe: $_____

Do you have any outstanding medical debt?/¿Debe cuentas médicas?

___ Yes/Sí ___ No

Amount you owe/Cantidad que debe: $_____

Do you have other debt(s)?/¿Tiene alguna otra deuda?

___ Yes/Sí ___ No

Amount you owe/Cantidad que debe: $_____

Do you have health insurance?/¿Tiene seguro de salud?

___ Yes/Sí ___ No

Do you have life insurance?/¿Tiene seguro de vida?

___ Yes/Sí ___ No

Do you use check cashing services?/¿Usted utiliza compañías de canje de cheques?

___ Yes/Sí ___ No

Do you use payday loan services?/¿Usted utiliza compañías de préstamos del día de pago?

___ Yes/Sí ___ No

Applicant Certification/Confirmación Personal

My signature below certifies that all information provided on this application is accurate and complete to the best of my knowledge./Mi firma abajo certifica que toda la información suministrada en esta solicitud es correcta y está completa a mi leal saber y entender.

Name/Nombre: _____ Signature/Firma: _____
Date/Fecha: _____

Authorization for Release/ Autorización para Publicación

I authorize Fondo Popular de la Misión (Mission Asset Fund) to photograph and interview me for use in a fund-raising video. I give Mission Asset Fund the irrevocable right to use my photograph and interview in this fund-raising video and all related print or video materials. The term "photograph" as used in this agreement shall mean motion picture or still photography in any format, as well as videotape, videodisco, Web, and any other means of recording and reproducing visual images and sound. I release Mission Asset Fund and its clients from all claims associated with these photographs. I acknowledge that this document contains the terms of our agreement, and I understand and agree to its terms./Yo autorizo al Fondo Popular de la Misión (Mission Asset Fund) para que me tome fotografías o a que me haga entrevistas con el propósito de utilizarlas en un video para recaudar fondos. Le concedo al Fondo Popular de la Misión el derecho irrevocable a usar mi fotografía y entrevista en este video para recaudar fondos y en todos los materiales impresos o de video. El término "fotografía" utilizado en este contrato, podría significar película o foto fija en cualquier formato, tanto como videocasete, videodisco, web y otras formas de grabación y reproducción de imágenes visuales y de sonido. Yo dispenso al Fondo Popular de la Misión y sus clientes de todas demandas relacionadas con estas fotografías. Yo reconozco que este documento contiene los términos de nuestro contrato, y que entiendo y acepto estos términos.

Name/Nombre: _____Signature/Firma: _____

Date/Fecha: _____

COMMUNITY DEVELOPMENT BLOCK GRANT (CDBG), CITY AND COUNTY OF SAN FRANCISCO: 2012–2013 FAMILY INCOME VERIFICATION FORM

Agency Instructions

1. Use the Family Income Verification Form Instructions to help with form completion.
2. Please complete and review this form with client.
3. This form must be kept on file for five years.
4. All items must be completed unless otherwise noted.

Client Information

Ethnicity:

(*Please also make a selection from the "Race" options in the next box*) Hispanic/ Latino(a):

___ Yes ___ No

Race

___ American Indian/Alaskan Native

___ American Indian/Alaskan Native and black/African American

___ American Indian/Alaskan Native and white (or "Mestizo")

___ Asian

___ Asian and white

___ Black/African American

___ Black/African American and white

___ Native Hawaiian/other Pacific Islander

___ Other or multiracial (please specify): _____

___ White

Family Information

A family is defined as all persons living in the same household who are related by birth, adoption, marriage, or domestic partnership.

___ Single female-headed family ___ Single male-headed family ___ Dual-headed family

No. of persons living in your family _____

Total estimated income for next 12 months for all family members: $_____

Optional Categories

___ Gay

___ Lesbian

___ Bisexual

Cultural Affiliation or Nationality (*please see instruction sheet and list of U.S. Census categories*): _____

Number of persons in "Family Information" must match this section. Circle correct income level. If number of family members is greater than eight, refer to instruction sheet.

Family of:	One Person	Two Persons	Three Persons	Four Persons	Five Persons	Six Persons	Seven Persons	Eight Persons
Extremely low income	$0–$23,350	$0–$26,650	$0–$30,000	$0–$33,300	$0–$36,000	$0–$38,650	$0–$41,300	$0–$44,000
Low income	$23,351–$38,850	$26,651–$44,400	$30,001–$49,950	$33,301–$55,500	$36,001–$59,950	$38,651–$64,440	$41,301–$68,850	$44,001–$73,300
Moderate income	$38,851–$62,200	$44,401–$71,050	$49,951–$79,950	$55,501–$88,800	$59,951–$95,950	$64,441–$103,050	$68,851–$110,150	$73,301–$117,250
Above moderate income	$62,201 or greater	$71,051 or greater	$79,951 or greater	$88,801 or greater	$95,951 or greater	$103,051 or greater	$110,151 or greater	$117,251 or greater

Income Certification

Interviewer: **Check** *the income level of the client and indicate below the source of information used to verify this information. Please see instruction sheet to help with completion.*

___ CalWorks

___ Food stamps

___ Medi-CAL

___ Tax return (*most recent*)

___ Unemployment (*check stub*)

___ SSI*

___ Payroll stub*

___ Other (*i.e., public housing/foster care*)*

___ Self-certified (*please explain*): _____

current with two months

I hereby certify that, to the best of my knowledge, the above statements are true and correct. I understand this information is subject to verification only by authorized HUD (U.S. Department of Housing and Urban Development)/CDBG officials.

Client Printed Name: _____

Parent/Client Signature: _____

Date: _____

Interviewer Printed Name: _____

Interviewer Signature: _____

Date: _____

Notes |

FOREWORD

1. IBISWorld 2018.
2. Consumer Financial Protection Bureau 2013a.
3. Consumer Financial Protection Bureau 2017.
4. powell and Menendian 2016.
5. Nonko 2016.
6. U.S. Department of Justice 2015.
7. Lawyers' Committee for Civil Rights 2017.
8. Lawyers' Committee for Civil Rights, n.d.
9. Faber and Friedline 2018.

PROLOGUE

1. Field notes.
2. Quiñonez 2015, 6.
3. Quiñonez 2015, 7.
4. Allen 2016.

INTRODUCTION: SEPARATE AND UNEQUAL

1. Bornstein 2014.
2. CFPB 2015, 16–17, 32; Avery, Brevoort, and Canner 2009; Pager and Shepherd 2008.
3. O'Brien and Kiviat 2018.
4. Fourcade and Healy 2013, 560.
5. Zelizer 2010.
6. Sen 1993.
7. Du Bois 1994.
8. Leyshon and Thrift 2007.
9. Somers and Block 2005.

10. Kear 2012.
11. Marshall 1973, 74 (emphasis added).
12. Honneth 1995.
13. Caskey 1994; Degenshein 2017.
14. Morgenson 2008.
15. Baradaran 2015.
16. Honneth 1995; Fraser and Honneth 2003.
17. Sykes et al. 2015.
18. Edin, Shaefer, and Tach 2017.
19. Consumer Financial Protection Bureau, "Consumer Complaints with Consumer Complaint Narratives," Complaint ID 2045739, https://data.consumerfinance.gov/dataset/Consumer-Complaints-with-Consumer-Complaint-Narrat/nsyy-je5y (accessed August 15, 2016).
20. Frakt 2018.
21. Marx 1975, 264.
22. Smith 1991, 388.
23. Douglas and Isherwood 1979. See discussion of how individuals manage the pressures to assist family and friends in Wherry, Seefeldt, and Alvarez, forthcoming.
24. Wherry 2017.
25. Pugh 2009; Zelizer 1994.
26. Robin Puanani Danner of Kaua'i, Sovereign Councils of the Hawaiian Homelands Assembly, quoted in Santos, Vo, and Lovejoy 2017, 6.
27. Cooley 1913, 198.
28. Cooley 1913, 200.
29. Cooley 1913, 203.
30. Hirschman 2013.
31. Zelizer 2010.
32. Zelizer 1994, 199; Borges 1994.

CHAPTER 1: THE INVISIBLE WORTH OF PEOPLE WITH NO CREDIT

1. Hyman 2011; Prasad 2012.
2. Quiñonez 2015, 23.
3. Daniel Lee, remarks at Mission Asset Fund's inaugural lending circles summit, Hyatt Regency, San Francisco, October 26, 2016.
4. Quiñonez, Pacheco, and Orbuch 2010.
5. Asoka Foundation, "José Quiñonez," https://www.ashoka.org/en/fellow/jos%C3%A9-qui%C3%B1onez (accessed November 5, 2018).
6. Millman 2013.
7. See Max Weber's discussion of Benjamin Franklin in Weber 2009.
8. *New York Times* 1919.

9. Smith, quoted in Klein 1992, 117.
10. *New York Times* 1922, 41.
11. Klein 2001, 331.
12. Brisco and Severa 1942, 156.
13. Poon 2007.
14. Poon 2007, 289.
15. Rosenberger and Nash 2009.
16. Rosenberger and Nash 2009.
17. Rosenberger and Nash 2009, loc 393.
18. Rosenberger and Nash 2009, loc 524.
19. Gödel quoted in Rosenberger and Nash 2009, loc 613.
20. Throughout the book, quotes represent individual statements by one interviewee, unless otherwise indicated.

CHAPTER 2: GIVING BROWN PEOPLE CREDIT: RACIALIZED HISTORIES OF MONEY, CREDIT, AND DISADVANTAGE

1. Burrell 2010, 4.
2. Nam et al. 2015.
3. Shapiro 2017.
4. Flynn et al. 2017.
5. King 1963 (emphasis added).
6. King 1968.
7. Vigil 1999, 60.
8. These struggles over the meanings of money and property had similarities between the Mexican-American War (1846–1848) and the U.S. Civil War (1861–1865). Tijerina advocated for the return of lands confiscated from Mexican Americans after the Mexican-American War. The Treaty of Guadalupe Hidalgo, which brought the war to an end, enabled the United States to take full possession of California, New Mexico, Nevada, Arizona, Utah, Wyoming, and Colorado and to ignore land titles held even by U.S. citizens of Mexican descent. At the time, Congressman David Outlaw of North Carolina, a member of the Whig Party, expressed relief that President James K. Polk was annexing only "the most sparsely settled part" of Mexico rather than the whole country "with its mixed breed of Spaniards, Indians, and negroes." Quoted in Holt 1999, 311.
9. Johnson 1968.
10. Reagan quoted in Carrillo 2008, 11.
11. Lotman quoted in Prasad 2012, 224.
12. Prasad 2012, 223.
13. Prasad 2012, 224.
14. Cole 1977.

15. Curry 2013.

16. Krippner 2017.

17. Husock 2008.

18. *Your World with Neil Cavuto*, Fox News, October 10, 2011, reprinted at Shepard 2011.

19. Barr and Sperling 2008.

20. Canner and Bhutta 2008.

21. Braunstein 2008.

22. Braunstein 2008; Federal Reserve 2008.

23. Yellen 2008.

24. O'Malley 1994, 381.

25. Zelizer 1994, 13.

26. Carruthers and Babb 1996.

27. Sumner 1896, 26.

28. Lincoln quoted in Office of Comptroller of the Currency, *Annual Report* (Washington: Government Printing Office, 1878), cited in Baradaran 2015, 36.

29. On the relationship between war and state-building, see Tilly 1990.

30. Pike quoted in O'Malley 1994, 379.

31. Paraphrased from O'Malley 1994, 379 (emphasis added).

32. Fitzhugh quoted in O'Malley 1994, 384.

33. Vickers quoted in O'Malley 1994, 378.

34. Penningroth 2003, 129.

35. Penningroth 2003, 129.

36. Penningroth 2003, 130.

37. Myrdal 1944, 929, 952–53.

38. Johnson 1934.

39. Harris 1979, 603–4.

40. Harris 1979, 614.

41. Harris 1979, 605 (emphasis in original).

42. Harris 1979, 614.

43. "Constitution and By-Laws of the Brotherly Union Society," April 1823 (Philadelphia: [printed by] William Brown, 1833), in Porter 1971, 58.

44. Midgley 2011, 19.

45. Hunter 2018.

46. Fleming 1906, 49–50.

47. Somers quoted in Fleming 1906, 50–51.

48. O'Malley 1994, 383.

49. Douglass 2006, 409–10. See also Harris 1968, 45.

50. Douglass 2006, 448.

51. Du Bois quoted in Harris 1968, 44.

52. Deposition from the Ho Report, no. 502, 44th Cong., 1st sess., 29, quoted in Fleming 1906, 58–59.

53. Hunter 2018.

54. William Lyon Phelps, "When Yale Was Given to Sumnerology," *Literary Digest International Book Review* 3(September 1925): 661, quoted in Hofstadter 1941, 490.

55. Compare discussion of the social characterizations of consumers in Wherry 2008.

56. Hofstadter 1941, 466.

57. Bonilla-Silva 2003.

58. Logue and Blanck 2008, 398.

59. Logue and Blanck 2008, 377.

60. Logue and Blanck 2008, 388.

61. Glaude 2016.

62. Zelizer 1994, 120.

63. Cited in Zelizer 1994, 122.

64. Ham quoted in Anderson 2008, 281.

65. Brody 2014.

66. Hochschild 1995, 15.

67. Kinder and Sanders 1996, 106.

68. Bonilla-Silva 2003, 6.

69. Mills 2000, 9.

CHAPTER 3: TURNING DISREGARDED PRACTICES INTO TRANSFORMATIVE TOOLS: MISSION ASSET FUND'S LENDING CIRCLES

1. The data presented in this chapter come from a number of different sources. Wherry made observations at MAF information sessions, meetings of lending circles, financial education sessions, and other events. He traveled to San Francisco fifteen times between 2012 and 2017 and visited for a minimum of three days and a maximum of twelve days each time. He took field notes, and his audio recordings of the information sessions that were open to the public allowed for verbatim transcription of some of the proceedings. Wherry also interviewed MAF staff while on-site.

   In the summer of 2015, our research assistant Marlene Orozco interviewed fifty-eight MAF lending circle participants. A recruitment email was sent to past and current lending circle participants noting that a $40 Visa gift card would be provided to anyone willing to grant a confidential interview. About 20 percent of the interviews were conducted in Spanish and the rest in English. Interviews were audio-recorded, although one file was corrupted and could not be used. We thus draw from the fifty-seven interviews that were successfully transcribed.

   The majority of the interviewees, 62 percent, were women. They were largely Latinx (53 percent), Asian (18 percent), black (5 percent), and unspecified or other (26 percent). The interviewees varied by age: 24 percent were between the ages of eighteen and thirty-five, 48 percent were between thirty-six and fifty, and the remaining 28 percent were over fifty. Among all lending circle participants, according to the organization's administrative data, 60 percent were largely Latinx, 12 percent were Asian, and 19 percent were African American. And the majority of lending circle participants, 64 percent, were women. When considering only MAF clients who took out their first lending circle social loan in 2017 at the Mission District office, we find a larger percentage of Latinx participants (64.5 percent), a lower percentage of Asians (13 percent), and a higher percentage of blacks (13 percent). In general, we wanted to interview a slightly smaller percentage of Latinx clients so as to include a wider range of ethnic groups in our sample.

The interview guide, which we developed in collaboration with MAF staff, covered perceived financial difficulties, experiences with mainstream and fringe financial services, financial goals, motivations for joining and experiences in the lending circles, and requests for financial help from network members. The semistructured guide allowed interviewees to discuss aspects of their financial lives that they believed were important while still covering the same set of topics across all interviews. On average, interviews lasted one hour.

Analyzing the data was a time-intensive team process. All the authors read over the transcripts numerous times and had frequent conference calls to discuss emerging findings. We also kept in frequent contact with MAF staff, talking through our initial findings and soliciting their feedback. For the analyses presented in this chapter, we primarily draw on interviewees' responses to a set of questions focused on their experiences with the lending circles, including how they learned about the program, how their circle functioned, what concerns they might have had about participating, and how they felt after they completed the circle. We coded responses to these questions in an inductive manner, looking for major themes that cut across the interviews.

Finally, we examined materials distributed by MAF to clients and the MAF website as other sources of information about the organization's approach to serving participants and rules about the program itself.

2. Field notes, January 12, 2013.
3. Mission Asset Fund, https://missionassetfund.org/programs/ (accessed May 30, 2018).
4. Translated from Spanish and paraphrased from field notes, January 7, 2013.
5. Lusardi and Mitchell 2014; Gale, Harris, and Levine 2012.
6. Bourdieu 1977, 166–67.
7. Karlsson, Loewenstein, and Seppi 2009, 97. For additional empirical verification, see Sicherman et al. (2016). For a general review, see the excellent article by Golma, Hagmann, and Loewenstein (2017). A similar argument on looking

at attention from the other direction and focusing on salience can be found in Stango and Zinman (2014).

8. Karlsson, Loewenstein, and Seppi 2009, 97.

9. We lack comparative evidence to ascertain the effectiveness of the financial management classes. It may be that the clients for whom the classes proved ineffective simply concealed their inability to benefit from them.

10. Field notes, January 7, 2013.

11. Field notes, September 16, 2013.

CHAPTER 4: BECOMING CREDITABLE, BEING AN EQUAL

1. The findings presented in this chapter are drawn from our fifty-seven interviews with MAF participants. We gleaned respondents' views on credit and creditworthiness, not by asking particular questions on that subject, but by looking for places in the interviews where respondents talked about it in the context of other questions. Drawing upon techniques presented in Charmaz (2006), we developed and refined a set of codes that reflected the main themes in those discussions.

2. Consumer Financial Protection Bureau 2013b.

3. Ludlum et al. 2012.

4. See, for example, Dahl 2004; Casey, Jones, and Hare 2008.

5. Federal Deposit Insurance Company 2009.

6. Servon 2017.

7. Halpern 2014.

8. Fourteen of the fifty-seven interview respondents self-identified as immigrants, and it is likely that more in our sample were born outside of the country. However, given the sensitivity of asking about immigration status, particularly for those who are undocumented, we opted not to ask participants directly if they were born in the United States or held a visa.

9. Low-income families may be eligible for other, in-kind benefits, such as child care vouchers or food stamps, but these benefits do not have the flexibility of cash. Moreover, many legal immigrant families are now ineligible for some public programs until they have resided in the country for a certain amount of time. Undocumented immigrants are not eligible for public programs.

10. Immigrants, both documented and undocumented, and particularly Latinx immigrants, are more likely than native-born workers to be employed through informal arrangements (Gentsch and Massey 2011; Massey and Bartley 2006).

11. Swift 2015.

12. Dvorkin and Shell 2016.

13. See, for example, Rohe, Van Zandt, and McCarthy 2001.

14. Seefeldt 2016.

15. Information retrieved from Trulia, "San Francisco Real Estate Market Overview," https://www.trulia.com/home_prices/California/San_Francisco-heat_map/ and http://www.mercurynews.com/2016/02/17/bay-area-housing-what-635000-median-price-really-will-buy-you/(accessed November 5, 2018).
16. Seefeldt 2016.
17. Interest on government-subsidized loans does not accrue if a candidate defers payment due to financial hardship.
18. Institute for College Access & Success 2016.
19. Seefeldt 2016; Halpern-Meekin et al. 2015; Hamilton et al. 2015.
20. Author's calculations based on data from the U.S. Bureau of Labor Statistics, http://data.bls.gov/cgi-bin/surveymost (accessed May 30, 2018), series ID: APU0000709ii2.
21. See, for example, Edin and Lein 1997; Sykes et al. 2015.

CHAPTER 5: CONCLUSION: WHAT WE MUST DO

1. Mark Schreiner and Michael Sherraden (2007) argue that the poor can save as well as their nonpoor counterparts, if only given an institutional chance.
2. Nam et al. 2015.
3. Shafir 2016.
4. Elliott 2009; Sherraden et al. 2007.
5. Hamilton and Darity 2010.
6. Wherry 2017.
7. Baradaran 2014; Wherry 2015; Servon 2017; Quiñonez 2015; Collins and Morduch 2011.
8. Mission Asset Fund 2014.
9. Balmert 2018.
10. Morduch and Schneider 2017, 177.
11. Santos, Vo, and Lovejoy 2017.
12. Hirschman 1970, 47.
13. Borges 1994.

EPILOGUE

1. Marquez 2017; *Denver Post* 2017.
2. Castillo 2017.
3. Associated Press 2018.
4. Wu 2017.

References

Allen, Danielle. 2016. *Education and Inequality*. Chicago: University of Chicago Press.

Anderson, Elisabeth. 2008. "Experts, Ideas, and Policy Change: The Russell Sage Foundation and Small Loan Reform, 1909–1941." *Theory and Society* 37(3): 271–310.

Associated Press. 2018. "Woman Arrested by Border Patrol in Front of Her Children Released by Judge." *Los Angeles Times*, March 21. http://www.latimes.com/local/lanow/la-me-woman-ice-20180321-story.html (accessed May 26, 2018).

Avery, Robert B., Kenneth P. Brevoort, and Glenn B. Canner. 2009. "Credit Scoring and Its Effects on the Availability and Affordability of Credit." *Journal of Consumer Affairs* 43(3): 516–37.

Balmert, Jessica. 2018. "Gov. Kasich Signed Payday Lending Law. What It Might Mean for Your Loan." *Cincinnati Enquirer,* July 23. https://www.cincinnati.com/story/news/politics/2018/07/23/what-ohios-new-payday-lending-law-might-mean-your-loan/792591002/ (accessed August 17, 2018).

Baradaran, Mehrsa. 2014. "It's Time for Postal Banking." *Harvard Law Review Forum* 127(February 24): 165–75.

———. 2015. *How the Other Half Banks: Exclusion, Exploitation, and the Threat to Democracy*. Cambridge, Mass.: Harvard University Press.

Barr, Michael S., and Gene B. Sperling. 2008. "Opinion: Poor Homeowners, Good Loans." *New York Times*, October 17. https://www.nytimes.com/2008/10/18/opinion/18barr.html (accessed October 25, 2018).

Bonilla-Silva, Eduardo. 2003. *Racism without Racists: Color-Blind Racism and the Persistence of Racial Inequality in the United States*. Lanham, Md.: Rowman & Littlefield.

Borges, Jorge Luis. 1994. *Ficciones,* edited by Anthony Kerrigan. New York: Grove Press.

Bornstein, David. 2014. "Invisible Credit." *New York Times,* October 2.

Bourdieu, Pierre. [1972] 1977. *Outline of a Theory of Practice*. Cambridge: Cambridge University Press.

Washington: CFPB (November 18). https://files.consumerfinance.gov/f/201311_cfpb_navigating-the-market-final.pdf (accessed October 25, 2018).

——. 2013b. "College Credit Card Agreements: Annual Report to Congress." Washington: CFPB (December). https://files.consumerfinance.gov/f/201312_cfpb_report_college-credit-card-agreements.pdf (accessed October 25, 2018).

——. 2015. "Data Point: Credit Invisibles." Washington: CFPB, Office of Research (May). https://files.consumerfinance.gov/f/201505_cfpb_data-point-credit-invisibles.pdf (accessed October 25, 2018).

——. 2017. "Financial Well-being in America." Washington: CFPB (September). https://s3.amazonaws.com/files.consumerfinance.gov/f/documents/201709_cfpb_financial-well-being-in-America.pdf (accessed October 25, 2018).

Cooley, Charles H. 1913. "The Sphere of Pecuniary Valuation." *American Journal of Sociology* 19(2): 188–203.

Curry, Thomas. 2013. "Remarks before the National Community Reinvestment Coalition." Washington: Office of the Comptroller of the Currency (March 20). http://www.occ.treas.gov/news-issuances/speeches/2013/pub-speech-2013-49.pdf (accessed July 22, 2016).

Dahl, Ronald E. 2004. "Adolescent Brain Development: A Period of Vulnerabilities and Opportunities: Keynote Address." *Annals of the New York Academy of Sciences* 1021(1): 1–22.

Degenshein, Anya. 2017. "Strategies of Valuation: Repertoires of Worth at the Financial Margins." *Theory and Society* 46(5, November): 387–409. DOI: 10.1007/s11186-017-9297-z.

Denver Post. 2017. "Melecio Andazola Morales Has Been Deported Despite Help from Colorado Congressmen, Loud Outcry." *Denver Post* (blog), December 20. https://www.denverpost.com/2017/12/20/melecio-andazola-morales-deported/ (accessed October 25, 2018).

Douglas, Mary, and Baron Isherwood. 1979. *The World of Goods: Towards an Anthropology of Consumption.* New York: W. W. Norton.

Douglass, Frederick. [1883] 2006. *The Life and Times of Frederick Douglass.* Hartford, Conn.: Park Publishing Company.

Du Bois, W. E. B. [1903] 1994. *The Souls of Black Folk.* New York: Dover Thrift Editions.

Dvorkin, Maximiliano, and Hannah Shell. 2016. "Why Did Loan Growth Stay Negative So Long after the Recession?" *On the Economy* (Federal Reserve Bank of St. Louis blog), January 11. https://www.stlouisfed.org/on-the-economy/2016/january/negative-loan-growth-great-recession (accessed October 25, 2018).

Edin, Kathryn, and Laura Lein. 1997. *Making Ends Meet: How Single Mothers Survive Welfare and Low-Wage Work.* New York: Russell Sage Foundation.

Edin, Kathryn, H. Luke Shaefer, and Laura Tach. 2017. "A New Anti-Poverty Policy Litmus Test." *Pathways: A Magazine on Poverty, Inequality, and Social Policy* (Spring): 10–13.

Braunstein, Sandra F. 2008. "The Community Reinvestment Act." Testimony before the U.S. House of Representatives Committee on Financial Services, February 13. Washington: Board of Governors of the Federal Reserve System. https://www.federalreserve.gov/newsevents/testimony/braunstein20080213a.htm (accessed June 7, 2018).

Brisco, Norris Arthur, and Rudolph M. Severa. 1942. *Retail Credit.* Englewood Cliffs, N.J.: Prentice-Hall.

Brody, Richard. 2014. "Coltrane's Free Jazz Wasn't Just 'a Lot of Noise.'" *New Yorker*, November 10. https://www.newyorker.com/culture/richard-brody/coltranes-free-jazz-awesome (accessed October 25, 2018).

Burrell, Tom. 2010. *Brainwashed: Challenging the Myth of Black Inferiority.* Carlsbad, Calif.: SmileyBooks.

Canner, Glenn, and Neil Bhutta. 2008. "Staff Analysis of the Relationship between the CRA and the Subprime Crisis." Federal Reserve memorandum to Sandra Braunstein, Director, Consumer and Community Affairs Division. Washington: Board of Governors of the Federal Reserve System, Division of Research and Statistics (November 21).

Carrillo, Jo. 2008. "In Translation for the Latino Market Today: Acknowledging the Rights of Consumers in a Multilingual Housing Market." *Harvard Latino Law Review* 11(1): 1–17.

Carruthers, Bruce G., and Sarah Babb. 1996. "The Color of Money and the Nature of Value: Greenbacks and Gold in Postbellum America." *American Journal of Sociology* 101(6): 1556–91.

Casey, B. J., Rebecca M. Jones, and Todd A. Hare. 2008. "The Adolescent Brain." *Annals of the New York Academy of Sciences* 1124(1): 111–26.

Caskey, John P. 1994. *Fringe Banking: Check-Cashing Outlets, Pawnshops, and the Poor.* New York: Russell Sage Foundation.

Castillo, Andrea. 2017. "Immigrant Arrested by ICE after Dropping Daughter off at School, Sending Shockwaves through Neighborhood." *Los Angeles Times*, March 3. http://www.latimes.com/local/lanow/la-me-immigration-school-20170303-story.html (accessed May 26, 2018).

Charmaz, Kathy. 2006. *Constructing Grounded Theory: A Practical Guide Through Qualitative Analysis.* Thousand Oaks, Calif.: Sage.

Cole, Robert J. 1977. "New Consumer Shields on Loans, Leases." *New York Times*, March 24.

Collins, Daryl, and Jonathan Morduch. 2011. "Banking Low-Income Populations: Perspectives from South Africa." In *Insufficient Funds: Savings, Assets, Credit, and Banking among Low-Income Households*, edited by Rebecca M. Blank and Michael S. Barr. New York: Russell Sage Foundation.

Consumer Financial Protection Bureau (CFPB). 2013a. "Navigating the Market: A Comparison of Spending on Financial Education and Financial Marketing."

Elliott, William. 2009. "Children's College Aspirations and Expectations: The Potential Role of Children's Development Accounts (CDAs)." *Children and Youth Services Review* 31(2, February 1): 274–83. DOI: 10.1016/j.childyouth.2008.07.020.

Faber, Jacob, and Terri Friedline. 2018. "The Racialized Costs of Banking." Washington, D.C.: New America Foundation (June 21). https://www.new america.org/family-centered-social-policy/reports/racialized-costs-banking/ (accessed October 25, 2018).

Federal Deposit Insurance Company (FDIC). 2009. *FDIC National Survey of Unbanked and Underbanked Households—2009.* Washington: FDIC (December). https://www.fdic.gov/householdsurvey/2009/full_report.pdf (accessed January 11, 2019).

Federal Reserve, Board of Governors of the. 2008. "The Community Reinvestment Act." Washington: Board of Governors of the Federal Reserve System. (February 13). https://www.federalreserve.gov/newsevents/testimony/braunstein20080213a.htm (accessed June 7, 2018).

Fleming, Walter L. 1906. "The Freedmen's Savings Bank." *Yale Review* (May and August). http://archive.org/details/freedmenssavings00flem (accessed October 25, 2018).

Flynn, Andrea, Susan R. Holmberg, Dorian T. Warren, and Felicia J. Wong. 2017. *The Hidden Rules of Race: Barriers to an Inclusive Economy.* New York: Cambridge University Press.

Fourcade, Marion, and Kieran Healy. 2013. "Classification Situations: Life-Chances in the Neoliberal Era." *Accounting, Organizations, and Society* 38(8): 559–72.

Frakt, Austin. 2018. "Kentucky's New Idea for Medicaid Access: Pass Health Literacy Course." *New York Times,* January 22. https://www.nytimes.com/2018/01/22/upshot/kentucky-medicaid-work-requirement.html (accessed October 25, 2018).

Fraser, Nancy, and Axel Honneth. 2003. *Redistribution or Recognition? A Political-Philosophical Exchange,* translated by Joel Golb, James Ingram, and Christiane Wilke. New York: Verso.

Gale, William G., Benjamin H. Harris, and Ruth Levine. 2012. "Raising Household Saving: Does Financial Education Work?" *Social Security Bulletin* 20(2): 39–48.

Gentsch, Kerstin, and Douglas S. Massey. 2011. "Labor Market Outcomes for Legal Mexican Immigrants under the New Regime of Immigration Enforcement." *Social Science Quarterly* 9(3): 875–93.

Glaude, Eddie S. 2016. *Democracy in Black: How Race Still Enslaves the American Soul.* New York: Crown.

Golma, Russell, David Hagmann, and George Loewenstein. 2017. "Information Avoidance." *Journal of Economic Literature* 55(1): 96–135.

Halpern, Jake. 2014. "Paper Boys: Inside the Dark, Labyrinthine, and Extremely Lucrative World of Consumer Debt Collection." *New York Times Magazine,* August 14. https://www.nytimes.com/interactive/2014/08/15/magazine/bad-paper-debt-collector.html (accessed October 25, 2018).

Halpern-Meekin, Sarah, Kathryn Edin, Laura Tach, and Jennifer Sykes. 2015. *It's Not Like I'm Poor: How Working Families Make Ends Meet in a Post-Welfare World.* Berkeley: University of California Press.

Hamilton, Darrick, and William Darity. 2010. "Can 'Baby Bonds' Eliminate the Racial Wealth Gap in Putative Post-Racial America?" *Review of Black Political Economy* 37(3/4): 207–16.

Hamilton, Darrick, William Darity Jr., Anne E. Price, Vishnu Sridharan, and Rebecca Tippet. 2015. "Umbrellas Don't Make It Rain: Why Studying and Working Hard Isn't Enough for Black Americans." Durham, N.C.: Duke University, Research Network on Racial and Ethnic Inequality (April). https://socialequity.duke.edu/sites/socialequity.duke.edu/files/site-images/Umbrellas-Dont-Make-It-Rain8.pdf (accessed October 25, 2018).

Harris, Abram Lincoln. 1968. *The Negro as Capitalist: A Study of Banking and Business among American Negroes.* Gloucester, Mass: P. Smith.

Harris, Robert L. 1979. "Early Black Benevolent Societies, 1780–1830." *Massachusetts Review* 20(3): 603–25.

Hirschman, Albert O. 1970. *Exit, Voice, and Loyalty: Responses to Decline in Firms, Organizations, and States.* Cambridge, Mass.: Harvard University Press.

———. 2013. *The Passions and the Interests: Political Arguments for Capitalism before Its Triumph.* Princeton, N.J.: Princeton University Press.

Hochschild, Jennifer. 1995. *Facing Up to the American Dream: Race, Class, and the Soul of the Nation.* Princeton, N.J.: Princeton University Press.

Hofstadter, Richard. 1941. "William Graham Sumner, Social Darwinist." *New England Quarterly* 14(3): 457–77. DOI: 10.2307/360486.

Holt, Michael F. 1999. *The Rise and Fall of the American Whig Party: Jacksonian Politics and the Onset of the Civil War.* New York: Oxford University Press.

Honneth, Axel. 1995. *The Struggle for Recognition: The Moral Grammar of Social Conflicts.* Cambridge, Mass.: Polity Press.

Hunter, Marcus Anthony. 2018. "22 Million Reasons Black America Doesn't Trust Banks." *Salon*, February 18. https://www.salon.com/2018/02/18/22-million-reasons-black-america-doesnt-trust-banks_partner/ (accessed June 7, 2018).

Husock, Howard. 2008. "Opinion: Housing Goals We Can't Afford." *New York Times*, December 10. https://www.nytimes.com/2008/12/11/opinion/11husock.html (accessed October 25, 2018).

Hyman, Louis. 2011. *Debtor Nation: The History of America in Red Ink.* Princeton, N.J.: Princeton University Press.

IBISWorld. 2018. "Financial Planning and Advice; U.S. Market Research Report." New York: IBISWorld (June). https://www.ibisworld.com/industry-trends/market-research-reports/finance-insurance/securities-commodity-contracts-other-financial-investments-related-activities/financial-planning-advice.html (accessed October 25, 2018).

Institute for College Access & Success (TICAS). 2016. "Student Debt and the Class of 2015: 11th Annual Report." Washington, D.C.: TICAS (October). https://ticas. org/sites/default/files/pub_files/classof2015.pdf (accessed October 25, 2018).

Johnson, Guy B. 1934. "Some Factors in the Development of Negro Social Institutions in the United States." *American Journal of Sociology* 40(3): 329–37.

Johnson, Lyndon B. 1968. "280—Remarks upon Signing the Consumer Credit Protection Act, May 29, 1968." American Presidency Project. http://www. presidency.ucsb.edu/ws/?pid=28894 (accessed June 29, 2016).

Karlsson, Niklas, George Loewenstein, and Duane Seppi. 2009. "The Ostrich Effect: Selective Attention to Information." *Journal of Risk and Uncertainty* 38(2, April 1): 95–115. DOI: 10.1007/s11166-009-9060-6.

Kear, Mark. 2012. "Governing Homo Subprimicus: Beyond Financial Citizenship, Exclusion, and Rights." *Antipode* 45(4): 926–46. DOI: 10.1111/j.1467-8330.2012.01045.x.

Kinder, Donald R., and Lynn M. Sanders. 1996. *Divided by Color: Racial Politics and Democratic Ideals.* Chicago: University of Chicago Press.

King, Martin Luther, Jr. 1963. "I Have a Dream. . . ." Speech delivered at the March on Washington for Jobs and Freedom, Washington, D.C., August 28. Washington: National Archives. https://www.archives.gov/files/press/exhibits/ dream-speech.pdf (accessed October 25, 2018).

———. 1968. Speech delivered to the sanitation workers striking in Memphis, March 18. http://nowcrj.org/wp-content/uploads/2016/10/King-Speech-Excerpts-1968-03-18-FINAL.pdf (accessed October 25, 2018).

Klein, Daniel B. 1992. "Promise Keeping in the Great Society: A Model of Credit Information Sharing." *Economics and Politics* 4(2): 117–36.

———. 2001. "The Demand for and Supply of Assurance." *Economic Affairs* 21 (1, March): 4–11.

Krippner, Greta R. 2017. "Democracy of Credit: Ownership and the Politics of Credit Access in Late Twentieth-Century America." *American Journal of Sociology* 123(1, June 29): 1–47. DOI: 10.1086/692274.

Lawyers' Committee for Civil Rights (LCCR). 2017. "Paying More for Being Poor: Bias and Disparity in California's Traffic Court System." San Francisco: LCCR (May). https://www.lccr.com/wp-content/uploads/LCCR-Report-Paying-More-for-Being-Poor-May-2017.pdf (accessed October 25, 2018).

———. N.d. "Not Just a Ferguson Program: How Traffic Courts Drive Inequality in San Francisco." San Francisco: LCCR. https://www.lccr.com/not-just-ferguson-problem-how-traffic-courts-drive-inequality-in-california/ (accessed October 25, 2018).

Leyshon, Andrew, and Nigel Thrift. 2007. "The Capitalization of Almost Everything: The Future of Finance and Capitalism." *Theory, Culture, and Society* 24(7/8): 97–115.

Logue, Larry M., and Peter Blanck. 2008. "'Benefit of the Doubt': African-American Civil War Veterans and Pensions." *Journal of Interdisciplinary History* 38(3, January): 377–99. DOI: 10.1162/jinh.2008.38.3.377.

Ludlum, Marty, Kris Tilker, David Ritter, Tammy Cowart, Weichu Xu, and Brittany Christine Smith. 2012. "Financial Literacy and Credit Cards: A Multi-Campus Survey." *International Journal of Business and Social Science* 3(7): 25–33.

Lusardi, Annamaria, and Olivia S. Mitchell. 2014. "The Economic Importance of Financial Literacy: Theory and Evidence." *Journal of Economic Literature* 52(1): 5–44.

Marquez, Viviana Andazola. 2017. "I Accidentally Turned My Dad in to Immigration Services." *New York Times*, October 24. https://www.nytimes.com/2017/10/24/opinion/ice-detained-father-yale.html (accessed October 25, 2018).

Marshall, T. H. 1973. *Class, Citizenship, and Social Development: Essays, by T. H. Marshall.* Introduction by Seymour Martin Lipset. Westport, Conn.: Greenwood Press.

Marx, Karl. 1975. "Excerpts from James Mill's 'Elements of Political Economy.'" In *Karl Marx: Early Writings.* New York: Vintage.

Massey, Douglas S., and Katherine Bartley. 2006. "The Changing Legal Status Distribution of Immigrants: A Caution." *International Migration Review* 39(2): 469–84. DOI: 10.1111/j.1747-7379.2005.tb00274.x.

Midgley, James. 2011. "Understanding Mutual Aid." In *Grassroots Social Security in Asia: Mutual Aid, Microinsurance, and Social Welfare,* edited by James Midgley and Mitsuhiko Hosaka. New York: Routledge.

Millman, Joel. 2013. "Immigrants Get Lending Hand to Get Legal." *Wall Street Journal,* January 23. https://www.wsj.com/articles/SB10001424127887323485704578256083335339360 (accessed October 25, 2018).

Mills, C. Wright. [1959] 2000. *The Sociological Imagination.* New York: Oxford University Press.

Mission Asset Fund. 2014. "SB 896 Passes! CA Becomes First State to Recognize Credit-Building." MAF blog post by lending8, August 20. https://missionassetfund.org/sb-896-made-happen/ (accessed October 25, 2018).

Morduch, Jonathan, and Rachel Schneider. 2017. *The Financial Diaries: How American Families Cope in a World of Uncertainty.* Princeton, N.J.: Princeton University Press.

Morgenson, Gretchen. 2008. "Given a Shovel, Americans Dig Deeper into Debt." *New York Times,* July 20. https://www.nytimes.com/2008/07/20/business/20debt.html (accessed June 5, 2018).

Myrdal, Gunnar. 1944. *An American Dilemma: The Negro Problem and Modern Democracy.* New York: Harper & Brothers.

Nam, Yunju, Darrick Hamilton, William Darity Jr., and Anne E. Price. 2015. "Bootstraps Are for Black Kids: Race, Wealth, and the Impact of Intergenerational Transfers on Adult Outcomes." Research brief. Oakland, Calif.: Insight Center for Community Economic Development (September). http://www.insightcced.org/wp-content/uploads/2015/07/Bootstraps-are-for-Black-Kids-Sept.pdf (accessed October 25, 2018).

New York Times. 1919. "A Hint to Credit Men: Regarding Credit Customers Who Keep Leaving a Balance." *New York Times,* June 1.

———. 1922. "Giving Warning of Credit Risks: Ways in Which Store Losses Are Prevented by Credit Men's Clearance Bureau." *New York Times,* September 24.

Nonko, Emily. 2016. "Redlining: How One Racist, Depression-Era Policy Still Shapes New York Real Estate." *Brick Underground,* December 29. https://www.brick underground.com/blog/2015/10/history_of_redlining (accessed October 25, 2018).

O'Brien, Rourke L., and Barbara Kiviat. 2018. "Disparate Impact? Race, Sex, and Credit Reports in Hiring." *Socius: Sociological Research for a Dynamic World* (May 3). DOI: 10.1177/2378023118770069.

O'Malley, Michael. 1994. "Specie and Species: Race and the Money Question in Nineteenth-Century America." *American Historical Review* 99(2): 369–95. DOI: 10.2307/2167278.

Pager, Devah, and Hana Shepherd. 2008. "The Sociology of Discrimination: Racial Discrimination in Employment, Housing, Credit, and Consumer Markets." *Annual Review of Sociology* 34: 181–209.

Penningroth, Dylan C. 2003. *The Claims of Kinfolk: African American Property and Community in the Nineteenth-Century South.* Chapel Hill: University of North Carolina Press.

Poon, Martha. 2007. "Scorecards as Devices for Consumer Credit: The Case of Fair, Isaac & Company Incorporated." *Sociological Review* 55(2, suppl., October): 284–306. DOI: 10.1111/j.1467-954X.2007.00740.x.

Porter, Dorothy, ed. 1971. *Early Negro Writing, 1760–1837.* Baltimore: Black Classic Press.

powell, john a., and Stephen Menendian. 2016. "The Problem of Othering: Towards Inclusiveness and Belonging." *Othering and Belonging* (blog), June 29. http://www.otheringandbelonging.org/the-problem-of-othering/ (accessed October 25, 2018).

Prasad, Monica. 2012. *The Land of Too Much: American Abundance and the Paradox of Poverty.* Cambridge, Mass.: Harvard University Press.

Pugh, Allison J. 2009. *Longing and Belonging: Parents, Children, and Consumer Culture.* Berkeley: University of California Press.

Quiñonez, José A. 2015. "Making the Invisible Visible: A Strategy for Inclusion." *Innovations Case Narrative:* Mission Asset Fund. *Innovations* 10(3/4): 21–33.

Quiñonez, José, Vivian Pacheco, and Eva Orbuch. 2010. "Just the Financial Facts, Please! A Secret Survey of Financial Services in San Francisco's Mission District." San Francisco: Mission Asset Fund. http://policylinkcontent.s3.amazonaws.com/JustTheFinancialFactsPlease_MissionAssetFund_0.pdf (accessed December 14, 2016).

Rohe, William M., Shannon Van Zandt, and George McCarthy. 2001. "The Social Benefits and Costs of Homeownership: A Critical Assessment of the Research." Cambridge, Mass.: Harvard University, Joint Center for Housing Studies.

Rosenberger, Larry E., and John Nash. 2009. *The Deciding Factor: The Power of Analytics to Make Every Decision a Winner.* San Francisco: Jossey-Bass.

Santos, Jessica, Angela Vo, and Meg Lovejoy. 2017. "Foundations for the Future: Empowerment Economics in the Native Hawaiian Context." Working paper. Waltham, Mass.: Brandeis University, Heller School for Social Policy and Management, Institute on Assets and Social Policy (IASP). https://iasp.brandeis.edu/pdfs/2017/FoundationsForTheFutureFINAL-min.pdf (accessed October 25, 2018).

Schreiner, Mark, and Michael Sherraden. 2007. *Can the Poor Save? Saving and Asset Building in Individual Development Accounts.* New Brunswick, N.J.: Transaction Publishers.

Seefeldt, Kristin. 2016. *Abandoned Families: Social Isolation in the Twenty-First Century.* New York: Russell Sage Foundation.

Sen, Amartya. 1993. "Capability and Well-being." In *The Quality of Life,* edited by Martha Nussbaum and Amartya Sen. New York: Oxford University Press.

Servon, Lisa. 2017. *The Unbanking of America: How the New Middle Class Survives.* New York: Houghton Mifflin Harcourt.

Shafir, Eldar. 2016. "Manipulated as a Way of Life." *Journal of Marketing Behavior* 1(3/4, February 24): 245–60. DOI: 10.1561/107.00000015.

Shapiro, Thomas M. 2017. *Toxic Inequality: How America's Wealth Gap Destroys Mobility, Deepens the Racial Divide, and Threatens Our Future.* New York: Basic Books.

Shepard, Remington. 2011. "Still Wrong: Crowley Revives Myth That Community Reinvestment Act Caused Financial Crisis." *Media Matters for America,* October 11. https://www.mediamatters.org/research/2011/10/11/still-wrong-crowley-revives-myth-that-community/182896 (accessed July 22, 2016).

Sherraden, Margaret S., Lissa Johnson, William Elliott, Shirley Porterfield, and William Rainford. 2007. "School-Based Children's Saving Accounts for College: The I Can Save Program." *Children and Youth Services Review* 29(3, March): 294–312. DOI: 10.1016/j.childyouth.2006.07.008.

Sicherman, Nachum, George Loewenstein, Duane J. Seppi, and Stephen P. Utkus. 2016. "Financial Attention." *Review of Financial Studies* 29(4): 863–97.

Smith, Adam. [1776] 1991. *The Wealth of Nations.* New York: Everyman's Library/Random House.

Somers, Margaret R., and Fred Block. 2005. "From Poverty to Perversity: Ideas, Markets, and Institutions over 200 Years of Welfare Debate." *American Sociological Review* 70(2): 260–87.

Stango, Victor, and Jonathan Zinman. 2014. "Limited and Varying Consumer Attention: Evidence from Shocks to the Salience of Bank Overdraft Fees." *Review of Financial Studies* 27(4): 990–1030.

Sumner, William Graham. 1896. *A History of Banking in All the Leading Nations,* vol. 1, *U.S.A.* New York: Journal of Commerce and Commercial Bulletin. Available at Online Library of Liberty, http://oll.libertyfund.org/titles/sumner-a-history-of-banking-in-all-the-leading-nations-vol-1-u-s-a (accessed October 25, 2018).

Swift, Art. 2015. "In U.S., Fewer Non-Homeowners Expect to Buy Home." *Gallup*, April 27. http://news.gallup.com/poll/182897/fewer-non-homeowners-expect-buy-home.aspx (accessed June 8, 2018).

Sykes, Jennifer, Katrin Križ, Kathryn Edin, and Sarah Halpern-Meekin. 2015. "Dignity and Dreams: What the Earned Income Tax Credit (EITC) Means to Low-Income Families." *American Sociological Review* 80(2): 243–67.

Tilly, Charles. 1990. *Coercion, Capital, and European States, AD 990–1990*. Studies in Social Discontinuity. Cambridge, Mass.: Basil Blackwell.

U.S. Department of Justice. 2015. "Investigation of the Ferguson Police Department" (Ferguson Report). Washington: U.S. Department of Justice, Civil Rights Division (March 4). https://www.justice.gov/sites/default/files/opa/press-releases/attachments/2015/03/04/ferguson_police_department_report.pdf (accessed October 25, 2018).

Vigil, Ernesto B. 1999. *The Crusade for Justice: Chicano Militancy and the Government's War on Dissent*. Madison: University of Wisconsin Press.

Weber, Max. 2009. *The Protestant Ethic and the Spirit of Capitalism, with Other Writings on the Rise of the West*, translated by Stephen Kalberg. New York: Oxford University Press.

Wherry, Frederick F. 2008. "The Social Characterizations of Price: The Fool, the Faithful, the Frivolous, and the Frugal." *Sociological Theory* 26(4): 363–79.

———. 2015. "Payday Loans Cost the Poor Billions, and There's an Easy Fix." *New York Times*, October 29. https://www.nytimes.com/2015/10/29/opinion/payday-loans-cost-the-poor-billions-and-theres-an-easy-fix.html (accessed May 20, 2018).

———. 2017. "How Relational Accounting Matters." In *Money Talks: Explaining How Money Really Works*, edited by Frederick F. Wherry, Nina Bandelj, and Viviana A. Zelizer. Princeton, N.J.: Princeton University Press, 2017.

Wherry, Frederick F., Kristin S. Seefeldt, and Anthony S. Alvarez. Forthcoming. "To Lend or Not to Lend to Friends and Kin: Awkwardness, Obfuscation, and Negative Reciprocity." *Social Forces*.

Wu, Gwendolyn. 2017. "A Dreamer's Best Friend." *San Francisco*, December 5. https://www.modernluxury.com/san-francisco/story/dreamers-best-friend-0 (accessed May 26, 2018).

Yellen, Janet L. 2008. Opening remarks to the 2008 National Interagency Community Reinvestment Conference, March 31. San Francisco: Federal Reserve Bank of San Francisco. https://www.frbsf.org/our-district/press/presidents-speeches/yellen-speeches/2008/march/yellen-opening-remarks-national-interagency-community-reinvestment-conference-2008/ (accessed October 25, 2018).

Zelizer, Viviana A. 1994. *The Social Meaning of Money: Pin Money, Paychecks, Poor Relief, and Other Currencies*. Princeton, N.J.: Princeton University Press.

———. 2010. *Economic Lives: How Culture Shapes the Economy*. Princeton, N.J.: Princeton University Press.

Index

Boldface numbers refer to figures, tables and photos.

homeownership, 91–93; mixed
realities of pursuing financial dreams,
90–91; remittances to family outside
the U.S., 95; student loans, 92–93
financial well-being: living with
dignity, 102–3; relationships and,
102; society's role in determining,
ix–xi; in the United States, ix
Fitzhugh, George, 51
Fitzpatrick, Michael, 2, 23–25
Fleming, Walter, 54
Follet, Earl, 35
Fourcade, Marion, 4
Frank, Barney, 48
Freedmen's Savings and Trust
Company, 54–57
free market system, social Darwinism
and, 57–58

Giron, Javier, 5
Glaude, Eddie, 59
Gödel, Kurt, 35
Gonzales, Rodolfo "Corky," 42

Halpern-Meekin, Sarah, 10
Ham, Arthur, 60
Hamilton, Darrick, 40, 100–101, 104
Harris, Robert L., 52–53
Hawaiian Community Assets
Organization, 14
Healy, Kieran, 4
Hilton, Conrad, 34
Hirschman, Albert O., 15
Hochschild, Jennifer, 62
holding money, 61
homeownership, 91–93
Home Owners' Loan Corporation, x
Honneth, Axel, 9
House of Representatives, U.S.:
Consumer Access and Inclusion Act,
hearing on, 22–26
Husock, Howard, 46

immigrants, 59–60, 88–90, 95, 113–14,
141n8–10
inequality: as the consequence of
conscious policy choices, 101–2;
credit invisibility and, 2; questions
regarding, xvi; the racial wealth
gap and the myth of a postracial
society, 39–40; unseen drivers of, 18.
See also credit justice; economic
justice/injustice
informal finance, 60–62
Isaac, Earl, 34, 38

Johnson, Lyndon B., 42–43

Kanungo, Mohan, 20, **121**
Karlsson, Niklas, 75
Kear, Mark, 6
Kinder, Donald, 63
King, Martin Luther, Jr., 41–42
Kiviat, Barbara, 2
Klein, Daniel, 33
Kohli, Shweta, **117**
Krippner, Greta, 45–46
Križ, Katrin, 10

Lacayo, Joel, 68–70, 72
Latinx. *See* Mexican Americans; people
of color
Lawrence, Merle, 26
Lawyers' Committee for Civil Rights, x
Lee, Daniel, 26
Legal Tender and National Currency
Acts of 1862 and 1863, 50
lending circles: as alternative financial
architecture, 65–66; checking accounts
required for participants in, 85–86;
described on the MAF website, 70;
financial education associated with,
71–73; financial education for
students, potential for, 85; formation
and participation in, 70–71, **118**;